JUST US

DAVID & JAN STOOP

JUST US

Finding Intimacy with God and Each Other

A DEVOTIONAL *for* COUPLES

Regal

From Gospel Light
Ventura, California, U.S.A.

Published by Regal
From Gospel Light
Ventura, California, U.S.A.
www.regalbooks.com
Printed in the U.S.A.

Published in association with the literary agency of Alive Communications, Inc., 7680 Goddard Street, Suite 200, Colorado Springs, CO 80920.

Previously published by Servant Publications as *Ten Minutes Together with God*. While the stories in this book are based on real events, they are composites. All the names and identifying details have been changed to protect the identities of the people involved.

Library of Congress Cataloging-in-Publication Data
Stoop, Jan.
[Ten minutes together with God]
Just us : finding intimacy with God and each other / Jan and David Stoop.
p. cm.
Originally published: Ten minutes together with God. Ann Arbor, Mich. : Vine Books, c2003.
ISBN 978-0-8307-4628-6 (hard cover)
1. Spouses—Prayers and devotions. I. Stoop, David A. II. Title.
BV4596.M3S764 2009
242'.644—dc22
2008039435

1 2 3 4 5 6 7 8 9 10 11 12 13 14 15 / 15 14 13 12 11 10 09

Rights for publishing this book outside the U.S.A. or in non-English languages are administered by Gospel Light Worldwide, an international not-for-profit ministry. For additional information, please visit www.glww.org, email info@glww.org, or write to Gospel Light Worldwide, 1957 Eastman Avenue, Ventura, CA 93003, U.S.A.

Contents

WHAT IS MARRIAGE?

DAY 1

Marriage Is a Covenant

And when I passed by and saw you again, you were old enough to be married. So I wrapped my cloak around you to cover your nakedness and declared my marriage vows. I made a covenant with you, says the Sovereign Lord, and you became mine.

EZEKIEL 16:8

Is marriage a contract or a covenant? When we look at how these two words are defined in the dictionary, the first definition for each word is the same: "an agreement between two or more persons to do or not do something specified." The other definitions offered by the dictionary don't give us much help in seeing how they differ.

Yet if we look back to Genesis 15, when God made his covenant with Abram, we can get a better picture of what constitutes a covenant. God's covenant with Abram seems very one-sided. God makes all the promises: to give Abram a multitude of descendents and to give him the land. Nothing is expected of Abram in return except that he be faithful.

On the other hand, a contract typically is a "this-for-that" kind of arrangement. The language of a contract states that if you do this, then I will do that—it is conditional. Furthermore, the two things exchanged are assumed to be somewhat equal in value.

Marriage is typically seen in our culture as a contractual arrangement—a "this-for-that." If one person doesn't keep his or her part of the bargain, then there is a problem and the contract can be broken.

For many, the marriage as contract has become very conditional. In other words, I as a spouse will do this for you, but in return you as my partner have to do that for me.

In our country, some states are trying to lower their divorce rate by offering two types of marriages: contract and covenant. If you choose the marriage as contract option, it can be broken, but the covenant marriage is for life and is taken much more seriously. That's the way God intended marriage to be—for life. His idea for marriage has always been that it is a covenant, where promises are made and kept unconditionally. Furthermore, if one side breaks a promise, God intends for us to be like Him and renew the covenant.

In Jeremiah, God expands on the meaning of covenant when we are told, " 'the day will come,' says the Lord, 'when I will make a new covenant with the people of Israel and Judah. This covenant will not be like the one I made with their ancestors . . . But this is the new covenant . . . I will put my laws in their minds, and I will write them on their hearts. I will be their God, and they will be my people' " (Jer. 31:31,33). A covenant marriage is a matter of the mind and the heart, not just a matter of the law.

Talking Together

Many couples haven't thought about whether their marriage is a contract or a covenant. Talk about your thoughts concerning this. If you do consider your marriage to be a covenant, how has that impacted your marriage?

Praying Together

Loving God, thank You for the covenant You have made with us as Your adopted children. We pray that You will enrich our relationship as we meet with You each day. Help us to give to each other unconditionally as You have given Yourself to us. Write deeply within our minds and our hearts the commitment we have made to each other.
Amen.

DAY 2

Marriage Is Blessed by God

*The next day Jesus' mother was a guest at a wedding
celebration in the village of Cana in Galilee. Jesus and his
disciples were also invited to the celebration.*

JOHN 2:1-2

Isn't it interesting that the first miracle of Jesus took place at a wedding? After Jesus turned the water into wine, the apostle John tells us, "this miraculous sign at Cana in Galilee was Jesus' first display of his glory" (John 2:11). We all love a wedding, probably because it is a celebration of the love between two people and it is an event where everyone can enjoy themselves. Yet, many times the bride and groom are too exhausted to enjoy the celebration. They may enjoy their wedding more later as they relive the celebration through photographs or a videotape.

Jan and I were married before the days when videotaping was common, so we relied on a good still photographer to give us a record of that beautiful day. However, we found we had hired a photographer who was not as experienced as he claimed to be. Halfway through the photos, he dropped his camera. He quickly checked it, but obviously didn't check it carefully enough, because none of the pictures came out. We were devastated, to say the least. So our wedding album is made up of snapshots that friends and family took. We are thankful that we have something we can look at to remind us of that day. Today, when we look at those pictures, we realize it isn't the quality of the pictures that is important; it is the memories those pictures stir up within us.

I know some couples who look at their wedding video or pictures every year on their anniversary. I think that's a good practice. It would help us remember a number of things. We may hear our vows again. We may see the friends who stood with us—maybe a large number or maybe just the two witnesses who stood up for us.

If you were married by a minister, you may remember the words spoken in the ceremony. You might recall the familiar reminder that "we are gathered here to unite this man and this woman in *holy* matrimony." Generally the minister then in some way describes how marriage was instituted by God in the Garden, that it was "adorned and beautified with his holy presence and first miracle." Sometimes the minister also refers to how Paul honors marriage by referring to Christ as the bridegroom and the church as the bride. What an important event a marriage must be in God's eyes!

One thing we can be certain of: God loves a wedding, and what He loves, He blesses!

Talking Together

Regardless of how big or how small your wedding was, it was a celebration. Maybe at your wedding something went wrong that seemingly ruined the celebration. Every wedding seems to have a story. What do you remember about your wedding? What were some of the things that went wrong? What were some of the joyful highlights?

Praying Together

Lord Jesus, we love it that You went to a wedding and that the miracle You performed there marked the beginning of Your ministry. Our wedding was important to us, and we know it was also important to You. Thank You for being there whether we invited You or not, because we understand marriage is so important to You. Thank You for caring about our marriage and wanting to bless us as a couple.
Amen.

DAY 3

Marriage Is a Holy Symbol

A man leaves his father and mother and is joined to his wife,
and the two are united into one. This is a great mystery, but it is
an illustration of the way Christ and the church are one.
EPHESIANS 5:31-32

The apostle Paul describes marriage as a "great mystery." How do two people become one, and yet remain themselves? It is a mystery! Webster defines a mystery as "anything that is kept secret or remains unexplained or unknown." Perhaps one of the reasons there are so many books written to help us with our marriages is that marriage remains a mystery. Who can explain what draws a man to a particular woman, or a woman to a particular man?

Whether I am a guest at a wedding or the minister marrying a couple, I always watch carefully to see what the bride and groom will do with the unity candle. I think the unity candle can be a beautiful expression of the mystery about which Paul is talking.

You probably know how the ceremony with the unity candle works. Just before the minister pronounces the couple husband and wife, they approach the unity candle. Each takes one of the individual candles, and then together they light the large central candle—the unity candle. This is a visual representation of the mystery of two being "united into one."

Yet that's not the part with which I'm concerned. I always want to see what they do with their individual candles after the unity candle is lit. More and more couples are leaving the individual candles burning along with the unity candle. When they do that, I almost want to cheer, for I think they have gotten it right. They are now united into one, but they are also still themselves.

I remember a wedding where, at the beginning of the ceremony, the mother of the bride and the mother of the groom each went up and lit one of the two candles at the side of the large unity candle. How appropriate—the ones who gave life to the bride and the groom "brought to life" their individual candles.

How can we be joined together in marriage, yet still be ourselves? That's a lifelong challenge that all married couples face. It's better than just becoming one, for then the question would be, which one of us will "we" be? Marriage doesn't dismiss our individuality—it's meant to enhance and develop it. That's part of the mystery of marriage—it is a holy symbol!

Talking Together
In what ways do you think that struggles with "oneness" could affect a marriage relationship? Can you think of incidences in your own relationship that might have been connected to the core issue of oneness versus your individuality?

Praying Together
Loving Father, Paul says our marriage is like Your relationship with the church and with us. How awesome that is! Help us to better understand that oneness with You. As we better understand how our marriage is a holy symbol, may we become increasingly aware of who You want us to be in our marriage.
Amen.

DAY 4

Marriage Is to Be Honored

Give honor to marriage, and remain faithful to one another in marriage.
HEBREWS 13:4

The writer to the Hebrews links together honoring our marriage and being "faithful to one another." He doesn't say we are to honor our spouse—instead we are to "give honor to marriage." Yet it seems that they do go together.

We watched Jan's mother deteriorate with Alzheimer's disease for almost ten years. For much of that time, she was completely unable to communicate. She became totally helpless and completely dependent on Jan's dad.

He put her in a nursing home at the beginning of the long ordeal, but he found that he was spending all of his time at the nursing home, and he was concerned about the quality of care she was receiving. So he brought her home, and for the last seven years of her life, he took care of her, along with a hired helper (who often wasn't much help). During those years, his life consisted of expressing his love for his wife by taking care of her even though she could not respond to his love.

Jan's dad showed his love for her and honored her as a person by doing this, but I think much of his motivation was that he was honoring their marriage. Over fifty years earlier he had made a solemn marital vow to her and to God that, no matter what, he would be there. He honored that vow. I think often of him and how he gave honor not only to the wife of his youth, but also to his marriage.

Sometimes as couples, we hit a snag in the road, and we may then find we don't even like our spouses. Some couples, in their anger with each other during those times, do foolish and hurtful things to each other and to their marriage. They forget the injunction that we are to "give honor to marriage" itself.

We are to take the very idea of marriage and place great value upon it. One of the definitions of the word "honor" is to "give weight to what is weighty." When we consider the importance God places on marriage, we know that any marriage is a very "weighty" subject—one worthy of honor. The blessing that comes from honoring our marriage is that we will remain faithful to each other.

Talking Together

What do you think might change in a couple's relationship if they put an emphasis on making the marriage itself the object to be honored as opposed to honoring each other? Of course, it is equally important that we "honor" our spouse as a valuable gift from God. Talk about what you might do or change in your own relationship that would show you are honoring your marriage.

Praying Together

Heavenly Father, thank You for the gift of my spouse.
Thank You that You brought us together. As we see more and more how important marriage is to You, we know that You honor it and we want to understand more fully what it means for us not only to honor each other, but also to honor our marriage. May we see that in doing this, we also then honor You.
Amen.

DAY 5

Marriage Is the Foundation of Society

Build homes, and plan to stay. Plant gardens, and eat the
food you produce. Marry and have children. Then find spouses
for them, and have many grandchildren.
JEREMIAH 29:5-6

It was Cicero who said, "Marriage is the foundation of society." We can take from that thought the idea that when a society honors marriage, its foundation is secure. However, when a society stops honoring marriage, its foundation will begin to erode.

Since 1960, the rate of divorce has accelerated to the point that approximately 43 percent of marriages now end in divorce.[1] In our culture there is also increasing pressure to broaden the definition of marriage to include same-sex relationships. Others seek to redefine the family unit, going way beyond the biblical image of a husband and a wife and their children. It seems that marriage and the family are under attack today, and it doesn't take any great leap of intellect to understand the truth of what Cicero said over two thousand years ago. Without marriage, culture will eventually erode and fail.

On the other hand, people still choose to marry today at about the same rate as they always have. It's true that a large number wait longer to marry, but marriage is still the goal. I was talking recently with a single young man in his thirties. He made no pretense as to being a Christian—in fact, his life revolved around a party lifestyle. Somehow the subject of marriage came up, and he thoughtfully said, "I think I'm about ready to get married. It's what I've always wanted. I want to have children and I want to find someone I could settle down with and enjoy for the rest of my life." His thoughts are pretty universal.

The prophet Jeremiah wrote to the Jewish exiles living in Babylon. He was urging them to establish themselves there and to "work for the peace and prosperity of Babylon. Pray to the Lord for that city where you are held captive" (Jer. 29:7). He wanted them to continue to function as a society, even in that strange land where they were held captive, and the way they were to do that was to marry, have children, and then have their children marry and have their own children. It's a universal truth. The quality of a culture is related to the value its people put on marriage, to being fruitful and allowing future generations to flourish.

Talking Together

In looking at Jeremiah's instructions, we realize that not all couples will have children. Some are waiting until later, while others are having difficulty with fertility. And others choose not to have children. If you do have children, how has that enriched and challenged your marriage? If you do not have children, how has that enriched and challenged your marriage?

Praying Together

Lord of all, we acknowledge our dependency on You,
both individually and as a couple. We are grateful that we as a
couple help form the foundation stones of our culture. Help us to
be faithful in passing on that truth to the next generations.
Help us to value our marriage in such a way that that value
can be seen by our family members and friends.
Amen.

Note
1. "Divorce Rates," Americans for Divorce Reform, Inc., http://www.divorcereform.org/rates.html (accessed September 2008).

DAY 6

Marriage Is Part of His Original Plan

Blessed are those who are invited to the wedding feast of the Lamb.
REVELATION 19:9

I don't think it is by chance that our understanding of marriage is under attack in our culture today. There is increasing pressure to redefine both marriage and the family, and the pressure is primarily oriented toward the diminishing of the importance of the marital relationship.

Some of the pressure comes from the realities of what is happening to families today. There is an increase of single-partner families. Researchers predict that within a few years, stepfamilies will outnumber non-stepfamilies. Nearly 40 percent of babies born today are born out of wedlock. And then there is the growing pressure for legal recognition of same-sex unions as constituting a legal marital relationship. Canada has already taken steps to finalize this redefinition of marriage. All of these changes contribute to a lessening of the importance and purpose of the marital relationship.

Much of this pressure is aimed at providing for a person's "happiness." Little is considered in terms of the consequences on the family, even though much of what has been taking place in our culture has led to dangerous increases in the types of problems we are experiencing with children and teens. God's plan for the primacy of marriage was to provide a solid foundation for the family unit—for the children.

If we turn to the early pages of Scripture—to the first two chapters of Genesis—chapter one gives us an overview of creation. Then chapter two goes in to greater detail about the events that took place on the sixth day of creation, and in particular in relation to the creation of man and woman. Before the sixth day of creation was over, there was a wedding! Marriage is a part of original creation! The final verse of chapter two states, "Now, although Adam and his wife were both naked, neither of them felt any shame" (Gen. 2:25).

Someone commented to me recently that God really must consider marriage important in that the Bible begins with a wedding and it ends with a wedding feast. John describes that feast like this: "Then I heard what sounded like the shout of a huge crowd, . . . 'Hallelujah! For the Lord our God, the Almighty, reigns. Let us be glad and rejoice and honor him. For the time has come for the wedding feast of the Lamb, and his bride has prepared herself'" (Rev. 19:6-7). Our marriages can be a foretaste of that wedding feast that is still to come.

Talking Together

In what ways do you see our culture trying to redefine marriage and the family? What have you seen happen to couples that have bought into these redefined roles? In what ways does your marriage reflect God's priority rating of the marriage relationship?

Praying Together

Dear Lord, we rejoice that You care so much about marriage. We are grateful that You care about our marriage. We recognize that there are so many demands on us— our work, our children, our parents, and even our friends—that we sometimes take our marriage for granted. Help us never to lose the sense of wonder, awe and mystery that surrounds our relationship as husband and wife. Give us the ability to keep our marriage number one.
Amen.

DAY 7

Marriage Is Powerful

For where two or three gather together because they are mine,
I am there among them.
MATTHEW 18:20

It's called "couple-power," or the "power of two." Pete worked with his wife in ministry. They felt like they were invincible—and they were. When hard times came and the church had to cut back on staff, they saw it as an opportunity to develop their own ministry. Together they are now carving out a new opportunity, developing supporters and creating a much-needed service for seniors. Those who know them are convinced they are an incredible team.

Tony claimed to be a believer, as did his wife, but they could never quite get in sync with each other. When his wife started a business that to her was also a ministry, he became jealous of the time she spent away from the house. When times got tough in her business, he withheld support, both financially and emotionally. Over the last five years they have grown apart, and now it seems like the only thing holding them together is their mutual resentment of the other.

Solomon talked about this when he wrote, "Two people can accomplish more than twice as much as one; they get a better return for their labor. If one person falls, the other can reach out and help. But people who are alone when they fall are in real trouble. And on a cold night, two under the same blanket can gain warmth from each other. . . . Three are even better, for a triple-braided cord is not easily broken" (Eccles. 4:9-12).

Both couples described here knew the Lord, yet only one of them spent their time and energy weaving together the "triple-braided cord," where they made Jesus an integral part of their plans and efforts together. Jesus has promised that where two of His children are together, He's there in their midst. This doesn't guarantee instant success in the way the world measures success, but our awareness of Jesus' presence with us as a couple does give us "couple-power." Perhaps that's why God made marriage His priority. He knew what could happen when a couple started working together with Him as a team. Like Pete and his wife, they would be unstoppable.

Talking Together

Pete's and Tony's marriages are probably examples of the two extremes—even though they represent real situations. Where would you put yourself between those two extremes? What are some of the things that would help you to work even better as a team? What are some of your strengths as a team?

Praying Together

*Almighty Lord, we want so much to be a team. We want to know
the reality in our marriage of the power of two, and even more than that,
we want to know the power of three when You are part of the equation.
Give us humble hearts that truly care for each other, so that we
can joyfully support each other's efforts.
Amen.*

GOD'S PURPOSE IN MARRIAGE

DAY 1

God Is Interested in My Marriage

And the Lord God said, "It is not good for the man to be alone.
I will make a companion who will help him."
GENESIS 2:18

The only thing pronounced "not good" in all of creation was man's aloneness. As God looked over everything He had created, it all was good. As Adam named all the pairs of animals, they were all good. Yet both God and Adam became aware that there was no one in all of creation who was to be Adam's counterpart, and God said that this wasn't good. Man was created to be in relationship.

In an age that has been characterized by a steep increase in divorce, people still want to be married. Especially men. It is a proven fact that men who are married live longer than their single counterparts. They are healthier and they are more content with their lives than are unmarried men. Marriage is good, and research suggests that this is especially true for men. God said it first—He knew it was not good for a man to be alone.

Yet, not too long after Adam and Eve become husband and wife, everything changed. It's hard to imagine how idyllic their situation was, up to that point. However, Satan tempted them, and they ate of the tree they had been told to leave alone. As a result, sin entered into their relationship. What started as a mutual relationship of openness and fulfillment became infected with fear, guilt and shame. When God confronted Eve, He told her that one of the consequences for their sin would be that she would desire to control her husband even as he tried to control her (see Gen. 3:16).

Because of sin, conflict and competition became a part of our marriage relationships. Yet that's not the end of the story. Once a couple finds the Lord and seeks to restore to their relationship the openness and intimacy that Adam and Eve shared together before they sinned, God is ready to help them achieve that goal. Thus, a couple can either live under the punishment of Adam and Eve with conflict or competition, or they can, with God's power, begin to build into their relationship the spiritual intimacy that any couple can share if they are open to God's working in their marriage.

God is interested in our marriages! He loves to redeem broken things. He loves to restore to His children what was lost in the Fall. Together, with God's help, you can build a marriage relationship that is growing toward what God intended in the first place.

Talking Together

Talk about how God is giving you as a couple the openness and intimacy that Adam and Eve must have shared with God before they sinned.

Praying Together

Father in heaven, we acknowledge that we are sinful people. Like Adam and Eve, we have been disobedient and know the feelings of fear and shame. Yet we also acknowledge that You have redeemed us through the shed blood of Your Son, Jesus, and so we ask that You help us restore to our marriage the joy and openness that Adam and Eve enjoyed before they sinned.

Amen.

DAY 2

Marriage Is God's Priority Relationship

And you husbands must love your wives with the same love
Christ showed the church. He gave up his life for her to make her
holy and clean, washed by baptism and God's word.

EPHESIANS 5:25-26

One of the word pictures that Scripture uses to describe the relationship a person has with Jesus Christ is marriage. In doing this, God shows us that He places a high priority on the marriage relationship.

Jan and I are often asked to teach in a cross-cultural setting. The class is made up of students from all over the world. When we talk about the priority of the marriage relationship, students from other lands describe the priority relationships in their cultures. Students from Asia talk about the mother-oldest son as being the primary relationship in a family. Students from the Middle East talk about the father-oldest son relationship as being primary. A student from Nigeria said that the primary relationship in his country was brother-brother. In Latin countries, it is the mother-child relationship that is primary. In many cultures, marriage seems to be secondary to a different primary relationship.

When we talk about the marriage relationship as being primary, the question is often asked, "Isn't that just an idea that is part of Western culture?" Our answer is an emphatic "No!" It is based on biblical principles, and yes, it is a part of Western culture. Yet it goes beyond Western culture, all the way back to the Garden of Eden.

If in God's order of relationships the marriage relationship is primary, then there are a number of implications that come from that principle. For one, we've found that when there is a problem with a child in the family, the problem usually is not with the child, but within the marriage relationship. Ken and Mary brought their sixteen-year-old daughter in for counseling. She was misbehaving and had run away from home several times, once staying away for three weeks. As we explored the relationships within the family, we found that the marriage was hanging together by a thread.

The only thing that kept mom and dad from getting a divorce was their "problem" daughter. When we dismissed the children from counseling and worked on the parents' marriage, the runaway daughter didn't need to be a problem anymore. Help had arrived. The obvious "problem" had been the daughter, but the real problem was within the primary relationship between mom and dad. The daughter, without knowing it, was being a problem in an attempt to save her parents' marriage.

Talking Together

In what ways do some couples place other family relationships ahead of their marriage relationship? Talk together about practical ways you as a couple can demonstrate to each other that your marriage is the top priority.

Praying Together

*Lord God, we want to fit in to Your biblical pattern for marriage.
We want to live out in very practical ways the fact that our marriage
is our top priority. We thank You that You value our marriage
relationship. Help us to be discerning of the subtle ways that we tend
to place other issues ahead of our marriage relationship.
Amen.*

DAY 3

God Himself Is Relational

For since we were restored to friendship with God by the death
of his Son while we were still his enemies, we will certainly be delivered
from eternal punishment by his life.

ROMANS 5:10

One of the mysteries about God is that He is relational. Relationships are so important to God that He sought to have a relationship with us humans even when we were still His enemies. He saw us when we were rebellious sinners, and because He longed to have fellowship with us, He solved the problem of sin by sending His Son to die for us. He loves us when we are good and when we are not so good. He loves us no matter what.

God's acceptance of us is our model for our marriage relationships. We are to love and accept each other no matter what. Sometimes we get caught up in loving and accepting our mates when they are good, and rejecting and withholding love when we see them as bad. Sid and Elise were caught in this pattern of dichotomous thinking. Each was convinced that he or she was blameless—all good—and equally convinced that the other was to blame for all their problems—all bad.

As they sat there in my office describing their marital issues, everything was in black-and-white terms. Each knew he or she was right, and each was working hard to paint the other as wrong. When we split reality into two absolutes, as Sid and Elise were doing, we blind ourselves to the real relationship issues because we no longer see the other person as having both good and bad within him or her. With that kind of thinking, a relationship suffers and both partners end up feeling alone and isolated.

The truth is that if God existed in isolation, we would have no model for understanding relationships. We would have no way of understanding how to love no matter what. Yet we know that the God of the Bible is unique, and His relational desires and experiences are an integral part of His character. God not only desires relationship with us as individuals, He accepts us and longs to deeply connect with us through our relationships, and primarily through our marriage relationships. In a human relationship, reality cannot be split into two absolutes. No one is ever all good or all bad.

The challenge of our human relationships is to move toward harmony. Experience teaches that harmony comes when we can see both the good and the bad in ourselves and in our partners, and accept that neither of us is perfect.

Talking Together

We all have the tendency to want to make ourselves completely right and the other completely wrong. When have you as a couple been caught in this trap? Are there any ongoing issues that make it difficult to see the other person's perspective? To break the pattern of dichotomous thinking, have a conversation in which you trade sides, discussing the issue from your spouse's point of view.

Praying Together

*Heavenly Father, we are grateful that You are relational, even
though we as humans cannot fully understand Your nature.
What we do know and accept is that You desire to be in relationship
with us. Thank You for fully understanding our human efforts to be
in genuine relationship with each other. Open our eyes to our blind
spots and give us perspective to see beyond ourselves.
Amen.*

DAY 4

God Is the Initiator of All Relationships

Then the Lord God made a woman from the rib and brought her to Adam.
GENESIS 2:22

There's a phenomenon that occurs during the fourth year at some colleges, called "senior panic." According to this phenomenon, if you're a senior and you haven't yet found your life mate, it's time to panic. Ray described how he panicked during his senior year and became convinced that somehow he had let the opportunity to find the "right" person slip by. He said that in retrospect he was glad his panic didn't push him into making a rash decision that he would later regret, yet he did wonder about some missed opportunities.

This was now ten years later, however, and he went on to describe how he had met his wife, who was sitting next to him. "After I graduated and realized I was still single, I was reading Genesis and was struck by the verse that says God 'brought her [Eve] to Adam.' God really caught my attention with that phrase, so I started to pray that I would have eyes to see when God 'brought' my wife-to-be to me. And I relaxed—the remnants of my senior panic faded and I really trusted God to bring someone to me. Four years later He did when He brought Libby into my life. When I first saw her, it was like He just dropped Libby in front of me and said, 'Here she is!'"

Libby wanted to interrupt and protest about the passive role Ray was describing for her, but he sensed that and went on to explain. "It didn't all just happen automatically, of course. I had to court Libby, and there were times when we broke up, but somehow inside of me, I knew Libby was a gift from God for me."

God is always the initiator. He initiated His relationship with us when He sent His Son to die for our sins. He loved us before we even knew Him. (See 1 John 4:9-10.) In many ways, God also initiated your meeting with your spouse. Our times are in His hands, and our meetings are coordinated by Him. What a beautiful picture of Eve being introduced to Adam, just as in some way you were introduced to your spouse. God is the initiator!

Talking Together

Talk about how you met each other. Who was introduced to whom? By whom? As you talk, consider how God was operative in that process of bringing the two of you together as a couple.

Praying Together

*Lord God, we are grateful that You are the initiator not only
of our salvation, but also of our marriage relationship. We remember
how we met and acknowledge that You were part of that process.
As You have brought us together, we ask You to walk with us,
as we are committed to staying together and honoring
You in our marriage.
Amen.*

DAY 5

God Is the Foundation of Our Marriage

God is our refuge and strength, always ready to help in times of trouble.
PSALM 46:1

There are a number of ways that couples connect with each other. Some couples connect intellectually and find that their most intimate times occur when they are in the midst of a heavy discussion on some intellectual issue. Other couples have built their relationship on their ability to work together. They may have started a business together and they now spend all their time together working.

Other ways of connecting include creatively, socially, and of course, emotionally and physically. One of the typical problems in a marriage happens when the husband approaches emotional intimacy through physical intimacy and his wife approaches physical intimacy through emotional intimacy. If we aren't on the same page in our foundation for connecting, we have a lot of work to do together to find a compromise.

Tom and Barb had built their marriage relationship on conflict. Yes, there is a form of intimacy that is based on conflict. It's often expressed in the saying "the fights are tough, but the making up is great!" Yet Tom and Barb fought all the time. They finally came to counseling when they became frightened that their conflicts were spiraling out of control. "We disagree on everything," Tom said. "We start when we get up in the morning and we don't stop until we fall asleep at night. If we have a spell without fighting, we don't know what to do with ourselves." Conflict was the foundation of their marriage relationship.

Studies have shown that couples that build their foundation on spiritual intimacy seldom get divorced. Only 1 out of 1,152 couples that pray together or read the Bible together daily will ever divorce.

That's less than one-tenth of 1 percent! If you are reading Scripture, or reading a devotional regularly, and praying together regularly as a couple—not just at meals—you are building your marriage relationship on a spiritual foundation. A marriage built on this foundation is rock-solid, even in the tough times.

Talking Together

Talk about the different types of intimacy mentioned here. Which have you experienced? What would you say is the foundation of your marriage relationship? If you say that God is your foundation, what are you doing together as a couple that is an expression of that fact?

Praying Together

Father, we want You to be the foundation of our marriage.
We want to enjoy other expressions of intimacy—the emotional,
the physical, the social, and the intellectual—but most of all we want
to experience spiritual intimacy with You together as a couple.
Help us to be disciplined in this way, that we together
might enjoy You more each day.
Amen.

DAY 6

God Is Our Love Teacher

Dear friends, let us continue to love one another, for love comes from God.
Anyone who loves is born of God and knows God. But anyone who
does not love does not know God—for God is love.

1 JOHN 4:7-8

No human knows how to love perfectly. We all struggle to some degree with our ability to love. Some of us love only conditionally. Others love too much and give themselves away in the process. We are all students in the school of love, and God is our teacher.

Rick was one who had a hard time loving someone else. He didn't think he had a problem with love, but his string of broken relationships made it clear even to him that something wasn't working right. Since our ability to love is set in motion with early experiences with the mothering figures in our lives, I asked him what his relationship was like with his mother. "Oh," he responded, "there never was much of a relationship with her. I don't think she knew how to love anyone. And when I look at how she was treated by my grandmother, I can understand why."

Rick went on to describe how all he could remember about his relationship with his mother revolved around losing something or losing someone he loved. He described how he came home from school one day to find all the neighborhood kids playing with his toys. When he asked a friend how he had gotten hold of his toy, he was told that he had found it in the trashcan. Apparently his mother had thrown out all of his toys, and the kids in the neighborhood had retrieved them just before the trash was picked up.

One of his stepfathers took a liking to Rick, and they developed a warm relationship. However, a year later his mother kicked the stepfather out and filed for divorce. She forbade him to come around or to contact Rick.

How can Rick overcome his deep fear that if he loves someone, that person will leave him? How can he really let go and love a wife? The answer for him, and for all of us, is to learn at the feet of Jesus—the love teacher. The apostle John tells us that "As we live in God, our love grows more perfect. . . . We love each other as a result of his loving us first" (1 John 4:17,19). Only as we allow God's love to penetrate our being and banish our fears can we truly love someone else.

Talking Together

Since all of us are students in the school of love, we all can grow in our ability to love. In what ways has God taught you through your marriage to be a better lover? Where are you still growing with regards to being able to give and receive love unconditionally?

Praying Together

Loving Savior, we come to You with hearts that want to love more perfectly. We know we can never reach that goal, but we want to learn from You, the perfect lover, how to love better, especially in our marriage. Teach us patience and understanding, and help us to always be aware of how much You love each of us.

Amen.

DAY 7

God Is Our Grace Teacher

Don't use foul or abusive language. Let everything you say be good and helpful,
so that your words will be an encouragement to those who hear them.

EPHESIANS 4:29

The old song says, "You only hurt the one you love." Unfortunately that is true in too many marriages. As I've worked with couples over the years, I've often wondered what would happen if a couple were to treat their friends the way they treat each other. At the same time, I've wondered what would happen if they treated their spouse the same way they treat their friends. We show a restraint with friends that is often missing in our marriage and family relationships.

I often teach a session or two in our church's premarital class. In that class I give the couples several "truisms." One is directly related to living gracefully as a couple. It goes, "There is no such thing as constructive criticism, especially in a marriage." In fact, I go even further and say that "constructive criticism" is an oxymoron. An oxymoron is a combination of two words that are contradictory, such as "jumbo shrimp." Even though we know what a jumbo shrimp is, if you think about the two words, it is like saying "big-little." In the same way, I see "constructive" and "criticism" as opposites when it comes to close relationships.

Some years ago I asked Jan to critique me whenever I preached or spoke somewhere. In other words, I asked her for "constructive criticism." She has been faithful over the years to meet my request, and to this day, I sometimes regret ever asking her. I thought I wanted to hear what she had to say, but I didn't expect it would feel like criticism. No "constructive criticism" rule is a principle that is even truer in the broad sense of our marriage relationship.

Even if we ask for the critique, it often feels like we are being attacked by our spouses, and we quickly go on the defensive. Paul urges us in all of our relationships to "let everything you say be good and helpful." We apply this verse, and others like it, to our general relationships, but what would happen if we applied this to our marriages? This isn't some Pollyanna approach to relating, only expressing the positive. It is instead a way of being careful to express grace to each other in the most important relationship we have—our marriages.

Talking Together

We often think we are being more "real" with those close to us when we can express ourselves freely. But according to the apostle Paul, that never gives us license to say just anything that pops into our minds. How would you characterize your manner of talking with each other? In what ways might you need to change if you were to literally follow Paul's advice?

Praying Together

Father God, we want to control our mouths. We want to live a life that expresses grace and mercy, not criticism and abusive language. We know that James tells us that the tongue is hard to control, but we want our marriage to be filled with grace. In those places where we struggle with criticism, give us power to be what You want us to be together.
Amen.

GROWING IN LOVE

DAY 1

Love Is More Than a Feeling

Love is patient and kind. Love is not jealous or boastful or proud or rude.
Love does not demand its own way. Love is not irritable, and it keeps
no record of when it has been wronged.

1 CORINTHIANS 13:4-5

Maybe you've read these verses over and over again and pondered them, especially in those early days of your relationship when love was so fresh and wonderful. You had this wonderful feeling about your mate and just knew that it was love. Yet, have you ever noticed that there isn't a feeling mentioned in the great love chapter, 1 Corinthians 13? Not a one! Love is described only as behavior.

I always cringe when I hear someone in a troubled marriage say, "I still love her (or him), but I'm not 'in love' anymore." Rather than get into a philosophical discussion about the differences in the two ways the person is describing love, I always say, "That's interesting," and then ask, "When did you *decide* to stop being 'in love' with your partner?" People usually don't know how to answer that question.

I go on to explain that love is a behavior. If it were just a feeling, how could Jesus command us to "love one another"? He said to the disciples, "I command you to love each other in the same way that I love you" (John 15:12). You can't command a feeling; you can command only behaviors. Look at the passage from 1 Corinthians 13 again. Can you see that it is talking about behaviors, not feelings?

So, first and foremost, love is a set of behaviors. When the behaviors of love are present in a marriage, the feelings of love will always follow. When the feelings of love fade, it means that the behaviors of love have grown cold or have been neglected. To bring back the feelings of love, or to maintain the feelings of love in a marriage, the behaviors of love must be present.

What often happens is that some of the behaviors we bring to our marriages that were once expressions of love begin to be taken for granted. There's nothing wrong with that—it happens to every one of us. What we need to do, however, is to continually find new behaviors that express our love to our partners. Never take love for granted. It's too precious a gift!

Talking Together

What are some of the behaviors you have used to express love to your partner? What things does your spouse do that make you feel loved? Share about other ways you could express love for each other through your behaviors.

Praying Together

Almighty Father, we thank You for loving us, and for giving us the ability and desire to love each other. Help us to always preserve our feelings of love through the acts of love that we give to each other. Give us the grace to follow through even when times are difficult.

Amen.

DAY 2

Love Always Follows Behavior

God showed how much he loved us by sending his only Son into the world so that
we might have eternal life through him. This is real love. It is not that we loved God,
but that he loved us and sent his Son as a sacrifice to take away our sins.

1 JOHN 4:9-10

Love is still an emotion, though. We don't take away the feelings of love by defining it as a behavior. The fact is, we can stir up the feelings of love through loving behaviors, and we can shut down the feelings of love through hurtful behaviors.

John didn't believe me when I told him this. He was convinced that even though he still cared about Sarah, his feelings of love were gone for good. I asked him if he would try an experiment over the next thirty days. To begin, he needed to make a list of at least ten positive things that Sarah could do for him that would show him that she cared. The items on his list had to be positive actions, something that Sarah would choose to do. They also needed to be little things that were very specific and observable. That is, by someone else who might be watching and could say, "I saw her do it. She did it!" I asked Sarah to make the same kind of list for John.

After they each made their list, they gave them to each other. The thirty days started at that point and Sarah was to do one thing from John's list each day—any one thing she wanted to do. Likewise, John was to do one thing a day from Sarah's list. All that either of them needed to do was acknowledge that the other person had done something from their list. It was interesting to watch John soften in his feelings toward Sarah over the next couple of weeks, and when the thirty days were up, John admitted that the feelings of love were stirring within him again.

The apostle John understood that unless love is expressed in action, the words of love have no foundation. He warns, "Dear children, let us stop just saying we love each other; let us really show it by our actions" (1 John 3:18). That's what God did when He sent His Son to be "a sacrifice to take away our sins" (1 John 4:10). He showed His love to us through His actions!

Every spouse loves to hear the words "I love you." Yet, even more important than the words are the behaviors of love. If you show your love through your actions, you will be surprised at the response.

Talking Together

Talk together about what would be on your list of ten things that you would want your partner to do for you to show that they really care for you. Or better yet, do what John and Sarah did and make your own list privately, exchange it, and each do one thing a day for your partner from their list.

Praying Together

Heavenly Father, together we thank You for showing Your love to us through Jesus' sacrifice for our sins on the cross. Keep us aware of the costly nature of Your love and help us to be willing to take the time and energy to show by our actions our love to each other.

Amen.

DAY 3

Love Needs to Be Spoken

*I have loved you even as the Father has loved me. Remain in my love . . . I have
told you this so that you will be filled with my joy. Yes, your joy will overflow!*
JOHN 15:9-11

We were presenting a workshop on marriage and had just talked about
the importance of our words as an expression of love. One woman
laughed as she raised her hand and said, "We've been married over
forty years and I don't think my husband's told me that he loves me
more than six times. What's his problem?"

Of course, he was sitting next to her, and after a moment he
spoke up and said, "I've told her seven times, and I can tell you about
each time I said it and why I said it." Everyone laughed with the couple as they enjoyed their candor, and then I asked him a question:
"How do you deal with someone who repeats something over and
over?" "Oh," he answered, "it's redundant and it drives me crazy!"
Then he went on to say, "I can't stand to be redundant myself and so
that's why I told my wife that I loved her when we got married and
that stood until I revoked it—and I've never revoked it. I see no reason
why I have to repeat myself."

Some people have a personality style that hates redundancy, and
to tell their spouses they love them every day feels unnecessary. In this
situation, however, personality must adjust; the words of love need to
be spoken as often as the listener needs to hear them.

As Jesus was spending His last evening before the crucifixion with
His disciples in the Upper Room, He told them He loved them.
He spoke the words of love at this crucial point, for He knew that in
the next days the men would be confused and discouraged. Yet He
spoke these words for more than just encouragement. He said, "I have

told you this so that you will be filled with my joy. Yes, your joy will overflow!" When the behaviors of love are present, the words of love bring overflowing joy to our hearts!

Find creative ways and places to express the words of love to your partner. Whisper, "I love you," in a crowd. Say it in front of your friends or family. Affirm the words of love in the midst of a heated discussion. If it feels awkward, say it until it feels natural. Everyone needs to hear these words.

Talking Together

Do you hear the words of love often enough? Are you comfortable expressing the words of love to your partner? Talk about how important the words of love are to you and about ways you can better express your love to each other.

Praying Together

Lord Jesus, thank You for telling the disciples You loved them.
We don't know how they felt about those words, but as Your disciples
today we are grateful for the assurances in Scripture that You love each
of us. Where we are uncomfortable giving the words of love, help us to
grow more comfortable. Where we struggle with receiving affirmations
of love, help us to open our hearts. Thank You for loving us.
Amen.

DAY 4

Love Can Also Be Tough

My child, don't ignore it when the Lord disciplines you, and don't be discouraged when he corrects you. For the Lord disciplines those he loves.

HEBREWS 12:5-6

There is a tough side to genuine love. This does not mean that we should discipline our spouse, though. If you want trouble in your marriage, treat your partner like a child. Why, then, have we chosen this verse and this subject as we look at love? The answer is, because there is a discipline that comes with love. When we truly love, we are going to encounter the tough side of love. Those times when we say, "No, I don't agree."

Some of us avoid this side of love for fear of rejection. "If I speak the truth, even in love, my partner will withdraw from me, and may even leave me," is the thought that races through our minds. Our fear keeps us silent. Then, slowly, resentment begins to build up within us. Eventually, a quiet bitterness begins to erode our experience of love as we emotionally withdraw into a place of isolation from our partner.

When couples avoid the tough side of love, research has shown, they eventually end up with an empty marriage where they feel like they have become two ships passing in the night. They lose touch with each other's hearts, and divorce is often the result.

Tom and Ellen were like that. They were married for twenty years and said they never had had a disagreement. All of their friends thought they had the perfect marriage, but now they were on the verge of signing the final papers for their divorce. Though physically present in the marriage, they had emotionally left the relationship years before, out of the fear of facing the tough side of their love for each other. Fearing rejection, they had stopped caring. They had never been really honest with each other.

How do two people avoid falling into that pattern? By being fully present, by speaking the truth in love, and by facing the fear of rejection. When two people truly love each other, and bring all of their personality to the marriage, there will be sparks. Honest feelings will bring conflict. That's the tough side of love, and every successful marriage can use those tough times to promote growth in both partners and in the relationship.

Talking Together

What are some of the subjects you think couples might avoid talking about in their marriage? When something is avoided, there is usually some fear that lies behind the avoidance. What are some of the typical fears that keep a couple from being fully present to each other in their marriage?

Praying Together

Lord God, we don't always want to face the things we fear, but we are also afraid not to face these things. We want to be like the Proverb, and sharpen each other so that we can become more like the people You want us to be (Prov. 27:17). Strengthen our love for each other so that we can find the courage to venture into those scary places.
Amen.

DAY 5

Love Is Gracious

Most important of all, continue to show deep love for each other,
for love covers a multitude of sins.
1 PETER 4:8

Perhaps the counterpoint to the tough side of love is grace. To better understand the apostle Peter's words, think back to the early days of your relationship—back to when your love for each other was truly "blind." Remember how gracious and forgiving you each were about each other's faults? However, the adage that "love is blind" seems to begin to fade in meaning sometime after the wedding. But should it?

As Peter wrote these words, he was reflecting on the verse in Proverbs that states, "Hatred stirs up quarrels, but love covers all offenses" (10:12). As a counselor sitting across from angry, quarrelsome couples, I often have had to remind myself that these people also love each other, or at least at some point in time they did. Yet right now they have forgotten how to exercise grace with each other.

When I first meet with a couple in my counseling office, they typically begin by talking about the problems they are experiencing in their marriage. Toward the end of our time together, I usually ask them a simple question: "How did you meet each other?" Almost every time, there is an amazing transformation in their emotions, in their attitude, and even in their facial expression. Prior to this question, they may have been angrily defending their position, and placing all the blame for the problem on their partner, but with this question, everything changes. Often they look at each other with a sheepish grin, as if silently asking each other, "Should we really tell?" Then they each describe their memory of that first meeting.

Then I have another question designed to help them remember what those early times—when the feeling of love was filled with passion—were like. I ask, "What really attracted you to each other at that time?" They are soon remembering the days when love "truly did cover a multitude of sins." I try to recreate in each of their minds the admonition given to the church in Ephesus in Revelation 2:4-5: "You don't love me . . . as you did at first! Look how far you have fallen from your first love! Turn back . . . and work as you did at first." Never forget the grace that filled your hearts as you felt those first feelings of love for each other.

Talking Together

Refresh each other's memory about the first time you met. What was it that drew you to your partner—what was so attractive to you at that point in time? Recall together how your feelings of love at that time were "blind"—how they "covered a multitude of sins."

Praying Together

*Loving Father, we confess that sometimes our love isn't strong
enough to "cover" what we see as offensive in our partner.
Restore to us the grace expressed in our first love for each other.
Then stir within us the energy and desire to hold fast to our
love for each other, never allowing our differences to
become a wedge between us.*
Amen.

DAY 6

God Demonstrates True Love to Us

Now, no one is likely to die for a good person, though someone might be willing to die for a person who is especially good. But God showed his great love for us by sending Christ to die for us while we were still sinners.

ROMANS 5:7-8

Larry was trying to put a positive spin on his statement that he wasn't "in love" with Kim anymore. He was talking about his "love" for her and his concern for what might happen to her in the future—a future that he saw as being apart from him. I let him talk, even though Kim had rolled her eyes in disgust at how he was rationalizing his attitudes regarding the situation. They were separated, and Larry had seen an attorney to begin the legal process of a divorce. As he wound down his "speech," he added, "You know, if Kim were in some kind of medical emergency, or any other kind of emergency, I think I would even be willing to die for her, but I'm no longer 'in love' with her."

I held up my hand to keep Kim from responding, for I knew she saw right through Larry at that moment. After some silence, I said, "Let me see if I understand you. You're saying you'd be willing to die for Kim, if the situation demanded that, but you're not willing to live for Kim anymore. I don't see where there is any love in what you are saying. I think you just feel guilty for what you are doing." Kim shook her head in silent agreement.

John writes, "This is real love. It is not that we loved God, but that he loved us and sent his Son as a sacrifice to take away our sins" (1 John 4:10). How did God love us? He loved us when we were totally unlovable. Paul uses four words or phrases to describe our condition when God chose to love us. We were "still powerless"; we were "sinners"; we were "ungodly"; and we were "God's enemy"—all clear examples of how unlovable we were! (See Rom. 5:6-11, *NIV*.)

Since we are called to love as God has loved us, His example calls us to love our partners even when they appear to us to be unlovable. John also tells us that loving the lovable is easy, but God calls us to love differently. We are to love as God loves, which means that we must love even our enemies. So, what can stop us from loving our partners?

Talking Together
Describe to your partner some of the ways you see him or her loving you graciously and unconditionally. When you experience their gracious love, describe what response you have within toward your partner.

Praying Together
Heavenly Father, we want to be able to love each other as You have loved us. Yet sometimes it is hard. It is beyond our ability to imagine how You have loved us so unconditionally. Our love seems so conditional, even though we don't want it to be that way. Help us to do more each day to love each other unconditionally.
Amen.

DAY 7

Love Is a Commitment

I command you to love each other in the same way that I love you.
JOHN 15:12

Remember your wedding vows? Some couples write their own and memorize them. Others repeat after the minister the standard vows couples have made to each other for who knows how long. A vow is a commitment. Webster says a vow is "a solemn promise, pledge, or personal commitment." In the case of wedding vows, the commitment is made not only to our partner, but to God as well.

Not many in our culture today value a wedding vow as a commitment. Some years ago, long before his death, I counted as a good friend the former president of Fuller Seminary. When I was a young pastor, he and his family lived just a few doors away from us. His daughter often baby-sat our three boys. I never met his wife—I don't really know anyone who did, for she suffered from a serious chronic illness. In all of her husband's presidential duties, she was absent, due to her health, and everyone accepted it.

One time, close to the end of his tenure, he wrote an article in which he became very personal regarding the commitment he had made to his wife—it was effective "in sickness and in health for as long as we both shall live." The point of his article was the value of obedience. He had made a pledge, and he intended to be obedient before God in keeping that pledge. That was the nature of Dr. David Hubbard—he was a man of integrity.

I remember a time when Jan and I were seriously at odds with each other. In the midst of our struggle, she said, "I don't know what you are going to do, but I'm going to try to be God's woman in this process!" It stopped me in my tracks. She knew what God expected of us both and she was dedicating herself to honoring that commitment.

The prophet Malachi told the people, "You cry out, 'Why has the Lord abandoned us?' I'll tell you why! Because the Lord witnessed the vows you and your wife made to each other on your wedding day when you were young. But you have been disloyal to her. . . . Didn't the Lord make you one with your wife? In body and spirit you are his. . . . So guard yourself; remain loyal to the wife of your youth" (2:14-15).

Talking Together

What do you remember about the vows you made to each other on your wedding day? If you have a video of your wedding, watch it again together. Discuss the meaning your vows had for you then, and the meaning they have today.

Praying Together

Father, there is so little in our culture today that reinforces the vows we made to each other in Your presence. Help us to rise above our culture and to continue to value what You value. Give us the strength to be faithful and obedient to what You have called us to as a couple.

Amen.

IMPROVING COMMUNICATION

DAY 1

Communication Is Listening

My dear brothers and sisters, be quick to listen, slow to speak, and slow to get angry.
JAMES 1:19

Have you ever really thought about how hard you have to work to really listen to someone? I often teach lay counselor courses, and a big part of their training is learning how to listen. Many of them, after the course, comment about how what they have learned about listening has helped their marriage relationship. They also agree that it is hard work.

I think the hardest group to whom I have ever taught listening skills was a group of Bible college students in Cambodia. After covering the material, I divided the class into small groups of three. One person role-played the one with the problem; one person played the role of the counselor, whose main task at this stage was to focus on listening; and the third person was to observe the process and comment on how well the counselor was able to listen. They did this three times, so each person got a chance to play the role of each position. Then, when we finished, we opened the whole group to a discussion about how well everyone had performed their roles.

With these young, energetic Bible school students, the discussion was very animated—and of course had to be translated to me. Yet most of the students wanted to argue against the need to listen. Their main complaint was, "We listen for a while until we know what the problem is, and then we want to talk and tell the person what to do." I can still see some of them standing up, trying to get that message through to me in a variety of ways, until finally my translator said something to them like, "We hear you, now stop talking all at once!"

Once it grew quiet, I asked them to think of what had happened to them when they were in the role of the person with the problem. I asked what their experience had been when the person who was supposed to be their counselor stopped listening and started problem solving. They became very reflective and then a number of them voiced their frustration with their "would-be" listeners. Several of them said that their counselor didn't listen long enough to really understand what they were saying, and they felt shut down. This made me think about all the times I have heard someone complain about the same behavior in his or her spouse—"He (or she) didn't listen long enough to really understand!"

Talking Together

The more we think we know our partner, the more we think we know what he or she is going to say before he or she finishes saying it. And sometimes we do. When have you been able to accurately finish each other's sentences? When have you thought you knew what your partner was going to say, but he or she said you missed the point? Which happens more often?

Praying Together

Heavenly Father, it is so much easier to talk to You than to listen, partly because we don't know how to really listen to Your spirit. Help us to become better listeners in our marriages, in our families, with our friends and coworkers. Most of all, though, help us to become better listeners to You, that we might really know and hear Your heart.
Amen.

DAY 2

Communication Is Speaking the Truth in Love

Then we will no longer be infants, . . . Instead, speaking the truth in love, we will
in all things grow up into him who is the Head, that is, Christ.
EPHESIANS 4:14-15, *NIV*

Sometimes it is easier to just "speak the truth" and let the chips fall where they may. Other times, we are silent because that feels like the loving thing to do. It really seems impossible to do both at the same time—to speak the truth in love. This is especially true in our marriages. It is often easier, and seems more loving, to just be quiet than to start trouble.

Mark had kept his mouth shut for several years. Liz had no idea what was going on inside of him. She had tried to get him to talk, but he kept reassuring her that everything was okay. Then, all of a sudden, he started talking, and Liz wished she had never asked. He had kept his silence he felt out of love, but now it was no holds barred. All of the resentments he had felt over the past years came pouring out of him. "I just couldn't keep it inside anymore," he told me, in front of Liz. "I started to talk and felt it was time to be honest, and, to tell the truth, I almost didn't care how she took it. I felt it had to be said."

How often that happens when we separate "speaking the truth" from "in love." How much better it would have been if Mark had not stored everything up inside and felt that he could not say what he needed to say. Yet like so many other husbands, he didn't know how his wife would take what he had to say, or he felt that talking would only make things worse, so he kept silent.

It's important to see that Mark isn't the only one at fault here. Liz probably played a part in what had gone on for years by overre-acting to anything Mark said. One reason it is so hard to tell the truth in our marriages is that when we hear the truth, it feels like our foundation as a couple is at risk. Nothing seems quite the same anymore. As much as we want to hear the truth, we tremble when it is presented to us. Our reaction can be just as important as what is being said. Of course, that's why what the apostle Paul says here is so apropos to marriage. When we speak the truth in love, we make it easier for the listener to hear what we are trying to say. We soften what we are saying, without changing its truthfulness. In a marriage, both partners must cooperate in order for either partner to really be able to speak the truth in love. Truthfulness bases a marriage in reality and trust.

Talking Together

Talk about how easy or how hard it is to discuss difficult subjects together. What makes it hard to "speak the truth" in your marriage? How could each of you help the other speak the truth more clearly?

Praying Together

Lord God, we don't want to shade the truth with each other, but we also want to know how to be more loving in speaking the truth together. Help us to be more sensitive to each other. Keep us from shading the truth as a false way of protecting our marriage. Give us the confidence that our love is strong enough to handle the truth.
Amen.

DAY 3

Communication Is Hearing Each Other's Hearts

But Jesus didn't trust them, because he knew what people were really like.
No one needed to tell him about human nature.
JOHN 2:24

Jesus had just thrown the moneychangers out of the temple area, and the Jewish leaders had come to question Him about His authority to do what He had done. He answered their questions and then He stopped, for He knew their motives. Jesus knew what was in their hearts. He knew because He was God in the flesh.

Often we think we know the motives that are hidden within the hearts of our partners. At other times, we wish our partners could read our hearts and minds in order to better meet our desires and needs within the marriage. Yet we are human and we do not always know what is in our partners' hearts.

"But he should know," Jenny protested. "He should just know what I mean!"

"Yet, he doesn't," I replied as I looked into Jeff's face, which was filled with frustration and despair. "He doesn't know your heart."

Part of Jeff's problem was that he kept attributing negative motives to Jenny's efforts in their marriage relationship. There were probably a number of reasons why Jeff felt that Jenny had improper motives for her behaviors, but the fact was that as long as he read her that way, he would hold back out of fear.

"What if you were to assume that her motives were pure?" I asked him. He pondered my question for a while and then reluctantly said, "It would make things better, I guess. But I'm not sure I can do that." Then he added, "I can try."

I'm sure that, early in their marriage, Jeff had been able to read Jenny's motives as more positive. So had Jenny read Jeff's more positively. But over time they had hurt each other too many times, and it seemed emotionally safer to assume the worst. At least then, they figured, they wouldn't be so easily disappointed. Yet in protecting themselves from disappointment, they also had pushed each other away, and the intimacy for which they longed became very elusive.

We need to be careful about expecting our partners to read our minds, but we should also be willing to risk reading the positive things that are in each other's hearts. Usually our partners want the same things we want in the marriage, and they are motivated by the same positive desire that we are.

Talking Together

We often talk about motives only when we feel threatened, or when things are not going well. Take the time now to talk about what might motivate your behavior toward your partner. In a positive way talk about what you desire from your marriage.

Praying Together

Heavenly Father, we are so limited in our ability to read each other. We want to know what is in our partner's heart and to hear and respond to what he or she longs for in our relationship. Yet we are often afraid to trust our partner's desires. Give us the courage to assume the best rather than the worst. Help us to remember times when we were able to do that, and how good it felt.
Amen.

DAY 4

Communication Is to Be Clear and Direct

"My Father will soon be dead and gone. Then I will kill Jacob." But someone
got wind of what Esau was planning and reported it to Rebekah.
GENESIS 27:41-42

Jacob had just stolen the blessing from his father that was meant for
his older twin brother, Esau. He had done this with his mother's help,
deceiving his father and pretending to be Esau. When Esau found out,
he was angry enough to kill. Yet he didn't tell his mother, nor did he
tell Jacob, his brother. That would have been an example of clear and
direct communication. Instead, Esau told someone who told someone who told someone who finally told Rebekah. That's circular communication, and it is not the kind of communication we need in our
marriages and families.

Sherrie described how her mother would call her when she hadn't
heard from Sherrie's brother. At some time during the phone conversation, her mother would simply mention the fact that her brother
hadn't called her for several weeks, and that she was worried. Somehow Sherrie knew that when she and her mother hung up the phone,
it was her task to check on her brother.

Sherrie would call him and ask him how he was doing and why
he hadn't called their mother. He would promise to call Mom, and
then, after their conversation was finished, she would immediately
call her mother to give her the report. No one had ever told Sherrie
that she was to do all this—she just somehow knew that was what she
was supposed to do.

The interesting thing was that when Sherrie's brother would call
their mother later that day or the next, neither of them would even
mention the fact that he hadn't called for several weeks. Nor would

Mom ever let him know that she was upset by his not calling. That problem had already been settled through their circular communication pattern. I wondered as I listened to Sherrie what would have happened if she had simply told her mom that she needed to phone her son if she wanted to hear from him. That would have allowed for clear and direct communication between them—a much healthier option.

Just as in our families, healthy communication patterns in our marriages call for clear and direct communication. It seems that we can best learn to communicate clearly and directly when we learn to change the patterns of unhealthy communication we have learned from our families-of-origin.

Talking Together

Every family practices to some degree circular communication patterns. Where have these patterns existed in each of your original families? How did you learn those patterns? What would happen if you broke those patterns and encouraged clear and direct communication in your family-of-origin? How could you help each other do this?

Praying Together

Lord, we want to develop healthy patterns in our marriage. We need Your help to do this, for it often means we need to develop healthier patterns within our families-of-origin. We know that You understand how difficult that can be, so we ask for Your help as we commit together as a couple to work on our communication patterns.

Amen.

DAY 5

Communication Is Hard Work

Let your "yes" be "yes" and your "no," "no."
MATTHEW 5:37, *NKJV*

Being a good communicator in our marriages is always hard work. There's just something about the nature of a marriage relationship that doesn't allow communication to just happen. What's so confusing about all this is that before we were married, we could probably talk for hours together and have no problem communicating. Then the wedding took place and we learned that we had to work hard at communication.

Part of the reason for this is that we are often attracted to someone with an opposite communication style. There are two basic communication styles. One we call the "literal" style and the other the "inferential" style. Literal communicators speak with complete thoughts and use periods at the end of their sentences. Inferential communicators speak with dashes, saying less than what they mean and assuming the listener understands what is being left out. The real problem occurs because we listen with the same style we use in talking. We are either literal listeners or inferential listeners.

For example, Patrick says to Erica, "Do you want to go out for dinner?" She answers, "No—" Patrick is a literal communicator, so he erases Erica's dash, puts in a period, and takes Erica's "no" as a fact. Yet Erica is inferential. Her "no" really meant "No, but . . ." Now here comes the work of communicating. Unless Patrick takes the time to find out what Erica really meant, he will be in trouble. She could mean, "No, I really don't know where to go." Or, "No, I think we've spent too much eating out this week." Or she could mean a number of other things that she just assumes Patrick understands.

Of course, the problem goes both ways. When Patrick says "no," he means only that, but Erica will assume that he means much more—after all, she means much more when she says "no." The work of communicating involves taking the time to let the other person know what we have heard and to make certain that what we have heard is what our partner really meant to say. The Bible says to let our "yes" be "yes" and our "no," "no," but then the real work is to make certain that our partner really heard what we meant.

Talking Together

Just about every couple experiences communication problems. What happened in a recent situation when you thought you had communicated with each other, but then found out you hadn't? To what degree do you think the problem was caused by different communication styles? What do you think would happen if you agreed to slow down in those situations and let each other know what you heard?

Praying Together

Loving heavenly Father, we struggle sometimes with really understanding each other. We long to hear our partner's heart and to understand what they are telling us. It seems so simple, yet it is so hard. Give us patience with each other during those times of misunderstanding. Help us to trust our partners more in this area, and to learn to listen with open ears.

Amen.

DAY 6

Communication Is Being Heard

*Anyone who is willing to hear should listen to the Spirit and understand
what the Spirit is saying to the churches.*
REVELATION 2:7

Quite often we think that unless we have arrived at agreement on an issue, we haven't communicated successfully. Recent research suggests that over our lifetimes as married couples, 69 percent of the problems we discuss will never be resolved. That may sound discouraging, but the good news is that 31 percent of the problems will be resolved. This statistic is true in both good marriages and failed marriages. Obviously, the difference is in how couples in good marriages handle the unresolvable issues.

There are three principles about communicating found in the passage from Revelation. First there is a willingness to hear, then there is listening, and finally there is understanding. Communication can break down at any one of these three stages.

Gary thought he was willing to listen, and it appeared that he was. As Meg talked about her concerns, he seemed to pay close attention to what she was saying. The problem came with understanding.

As soon as Meg took a breath, Gary jumped in with his counterargument. He was intent on showing that Meg was wrong in what she was saying. I stopped him and asked if he thought he had really heard what Meg had said. He was able to repeat it almost word for word! Before he could jump in with his counterargument again, however, I asked him what he thought Meg had meant by what she had said. He stopped talking, and you could almost see the wheels turning in his mind as he went over the words he had heard. Then he said, "I guess I just don't get it. I don't understand what she's trying to get at."

Meg let out a sigh of relief as she said, "I know. That's what I keep saying—you just don't understand what I'm trying to say."

"But I don't agree with you," was Gary's response. That's when I jumped in and pointed out that he didn't need to agree with what she was saying in order to understand. Yet until he could let her know that he understood what she was saying, his disagreement only worsened the situation. Understanding isn't the same as agreement.

Talking Together

Sometimes we are so set on reaching agreement that we forget to try and understand our partner. Can you think of situations where either of you skipped over the understanding part? What blocked your ability to communicate understanding in those situations? How could you do things differently in the future in order to better communicate understanding?

Praying Together

Father, we confess that we struggle at times with a willingness to listen, but we also struggle with understanding. We need Your help so that we can be more patient with each other in this area. Help us to let go of the need to be in agreement so that we can better work at understanding each other.
Amen.

DAY 7

Communication Can Occur–Even in Caves

"Yes, go. But tell my people this: 'You will hear my words, but you will not understand. You will see what I do, but you will not perceive its meaning.'"
ISAIAH 6:9

God's call to Isaiah was a call to a very frustrating, almost hopeless task. As he listened to God's instructions, he lamented, "Lord, how long must I do this?" God's answer to Isaiah was even more discouraging: he was to do this until all was destroyed. Isaiah was being told what would happen when he prophesied what God had told him to prophesy. Yet God could also have been describing what happens when couples try to communicate. They will hear the words, but won't understand.

One writer, in describing the typical interaction between a husband and a wife, said that husbands have a need to retreat to their "caves." The implication is that once he is in his cave, communication is lost. Yet I've found that communication between a husband and a wife can take place even in this cave. Here's how.

Darin and Tami were talking about their marital issues—or, I should say, Tami was talking. After several minutes, I asked Darin what he thought about what his wife was saying. As he took a moment to reflect on my question, Tami started to answer for him. I held up my hand and said to her, "Wait. I want to hear what Darin is thinking."

Finally, he started talking. He hesitated often as he talked, as if he was letting his brain and his mouth get in sync with each other. Several times during his momentary hesitations, Tami tried to jump in and talk for him. She was struggling with the slowness of his response. Darin continued talking, and Tami was surprised at some of the things she heard him say. She received some new insights and gained a more positive understanding about his commitment to their marriage relationship.

Several times during our meeting I had to ask Tami to wait and let Darin talk. Finally she said, "He talks more here in your office than he ever talks anyplace else." I wanted to say something like, "That's because I won't let you talk for him," but decided to say, "You need to learn to wait and let him talk. You might try counting to twenty-five silently when you get frustrated with the slowness of his comments." After all, that's what Jan does with me. It often works—I do respond eventually.

Talking Together

Which one of you tends to retreat inside of yourself at times? What changes in your relationship when this happens? What could you do differently in the future to ensure that communication does not stop when one is processing internally?

Praying Together

Lord, we are so different, and most of the time we like our differences. Yet we need Your help in those times when we misunderstand each other's behaviors. Give us hearts full of grace for our partners. Help us to respect each other's differences. As we show that grace, help us to have ears that hear and eyes that see all the good things You have in store for us and for our marriage.
Amen.

FINDING INTIMACY

DAY 1

Intimacy Is Multifaceted

*Always keep yourselves united in the Holy Spirit,
and bind yourselves together with peace.*
EPHESIANS 4:3

Men and women typically differ from each other in the way they understand and use the term "intimacy." What is interesting is that they have probably heard each other's definition of the word hundreds of times, yet they still think their partner means the same thing they themselves mean when they use the word. A conversation can go like this:

He: We need more intimacy (sex) in our marriage.

She: We sure do, but every time I try to be intimate (emotionally) with you, you clam up.

He: What do you mean I clam up? I'm the one who wants intimacy (sex).

She: Oh, really? You don't even know what the word means.

And on it goes. At some level they each know what the other is talking about, but when the discussion about intimacy gets started, each assumes his or her own definition is common to them both.

Obviously, both types of intimacy referred to here are a part of what constitutes intimacy. A more general definition could be similar to what Paul said to the Ephesians when he wrote, "Bind yourselves together with peace." Intimacy in a marriage is a "binding together" activity, and includes the physical act of sex and also the emotional bond that is so necessary for a marriage to be satisfying.

In truth, intimacy is even more than physical or emotional closeness. It is multifaceted, and a healthy, growing marriage will be seeking to experience the whole spectrum of intimacy. In addition to physical and emotional intimacy, couples need to experience the closeness that comes from doing things together socially, working together on a project, participating in intellectual discussions, and even experiencing conflict. The aspect of intimacy that most couples miss is the closeness they can experience by walking together spiritually. If any of these areas of intimacy are missing, however, a marriage can be like driving on a tire with a permanent flat spot—a very bumpy ride.

Talking Together

It's hard to keep all these areas of intimacy working, and impossible to keep them working at the same time. But the concern is the neglect of any area. What areas of intimacy do you often share comfortably? What areas are difficult for you as a couple? What one thing might you do to improve the quality of your intimacy?

Praying Together

Loving Father, we know You care about us as a couple and want us to share a binding together in love and peace. Sometimes our binding together is anything but peaceful, and we need Your help to get on track. Help us especially in the area of spiritual intimacy. We want to learn how as a couple we can know You better.
Amen.

DAY 2

Finding Spiritual Intimacy

Then God will rejoice over you as a bridegroom rejoices over his bride.
ISAIAH 62:5

Statistics show that the foundation for all areas of intimacy needs to be spiritual intimacy. We have all heard that the divorce rate in our country is somewhere around 50 percent, which means that while there are 2.3 million marriages a year, there are also 1.15 million divorces a year. The statistic we seldom, if ever, hear, and that bears repeating from an earlier devotional, is that when a couple works on developing spiritual intimacy, especially through reading the Bible together and praying together daily, the divorce rate drops to less than 0.1 percent. Pretty amazing!

During the early years of our marriage, we struggled with the issue of developing spiritual intimacy. Jan wanted us to pray together as a couple, and I was resistant. I was a pastor at that time, and I could pray with people in my office, I could pray in front of a Sunday school class, and I could even pray in front of the whole congregation. I could pray with my family—but it was too scary for me to pray just with Jan.

I think I was afraid that she would get to know some part of me that she wouldn't like, for I was convinced that praying with your wife meant you talked to God in front of her about all your hidden struggles. I don't know where that idea came from, but I know that is what I felt. I wasn't alone in that struggle, apparently, for only about 4 percent of all Christian couples actually pray together on a daily basis.

Jan didn't give up, though, and in about the tenth year of our marriage I "bit the bullet" and said, "Okay, let's start praying together." For over thirty-five years now we have seldom missed a night of praying together. I am writing this while I am on a teaching mission in South

Korea. Jan is at home. Yet, as we do any time we are apart, we have arranged to talk to each other each day, and we spend part of that time praying together.

We often pray for the same things—our kids, our extended family, our friends, and any special needs they might represent. We've talked about whether we bore God with our prayers. We think not. It's something like what happens when one of our grandchildren crawls up in our laps and talks to us about the same thing he or she talked to us about the last time we saw him or her. We're not bored—we love the intimacy. And somehow we believe that when we crawl up in God's lap, He's never bored. He loves the intimacy even more than we do.

Talking Together

We hope you have started to pray together as you are reading this devotional. If it's been hard for you to do that part, talk about some of the reasons. Why do you think it's hard for couples to pray together? What made it difficult for you to start? If you are already praying together, what has become most meaningful to you in praying together?

Praying Together

*Almighty Lord, we know how important it is for us as a couple
to come together into Your presence. We thank You for wanting
to meet with us. We know how important it is for us to pray
individually, but we also want to experience You more as a couple.
Help us be consistent in praying together. We pray that we
may experience great joy together in Your presence.*
Amen.

DAY 3
Enjoying Physical Intimacy

*The husband should not deprive his wife of sexual intimacy, which is her right
as a married woman, nor should the wife deprive her husband.*
1 CORINTHIANS 7:3

It's interesting that Paul is talking primarily to husbands here, and
seems to add his advice to the wife only as an afterthought. The way
men talk about sex, one would think that Paul's main admonition
would be to the wives. Yet it's to the husbands.

In some ways, I believe that our culture's emphasis on sex is deceiving. Men act interested in sex, but when it comes right down to it,
I've found that with most couples it is the wife who complains about
the lack of sex in their marriage. Here's a conversation that I often
hear in my office: Ed and Jane were talking about the lack of intimacy
in their marriage when Jane said, "He only seems to want to talk
about our lack of sex—he doesn't really want to do anything about it.
There have been many nights when I've hinted that I was ready to
make love, and he's found some excuse to stay up late and avoid me."

Ed's response was quick and defensive. "What do you mean?
When have you hinted that you were interested? If you've hinted, the
hints were too subtle for anyone to pick up. I just don't think you're
interested." Jane listened quietly and then began to list for him what
had happened each night over the past two weeks—how he had found
some reason to stay up after Jane had gone to bed.

Jane's experience isn't that uncommon. Having a good physical
relationship takes time, and men are often impatient with the process. Men will sometimes want to use sex as a way to reassure themselves after an argument that everything is okay in their marriage. Or
they may just want to have sex in order to satisfy their own physical

needs. Usually, neither of these approaches considers the investment of time and energy it takes to develop true physical intimacy.

I have found that good sex is the result of good communication. Couples who really enjoy the physical side of their marriage have learned not only how to talk to each other, but also how to talk to each other about the subject of sex. It makes for a very stimulating conversation.

Talking Together

How easy is it for you to talk to each other about sex? When was the last time you had an in-depth conversation about the physical part of your marriage? Take the time now to talk about how you feel about your sexual relationship.

Praying Together

Lord, You are the Creator of our sexuality. It is a part of
Your creation that You felt good about. We are grateful that
You enjoyed making us sexual beings. Help us to understand more
and more how we can enjoy that part of our relationship.
Thank You for blessing the sexual part of our marriage.
Amen.

DAY 4

Developing Emotional Intimacy

He comforts us in all our troubles so that we can comfort others. When others are
troubled, we will be able to give them the same comfort God has given us.
2 CORINTHIANS 1:4

Every couple comes to marriage with a desire and an expectation for
emotional closeness. We all have high hopes that somehow we will become soul mates. There is nothing wrong with that expectation, but
all too many couples fall short of their hopes. That's where Ed and
Jane were. Jane felt she had lowered her expectations regarding emotional closeness with Ed. She had gone through a period of grieving
over what she believed would never happen in her marriage. As she
talked about her sadness over this, Ed was visibly moved. His whole
demeanor softened.

"You know, I wanted that emotional closeness as well," he finally
said. "But I guess I just didn't know how to get it, or I was afraid to try."

Jane's response wasn't what he expected, as she pointed out, "You
know, it wouldn't be that hard for us to still accomplish what we both
seem to want. Can we talk about what we expect from each other?"

As the conversation continued, what Jane pointed out were little
things that could make a tremendous difference. Things like showing an
interest in how she was feeling, or asking about her day, or taking out
the trash without having to be asked. She added, "I don't need you to sit
down with me for hours and share your deepest issues with me—that
would probably be too scary for me, too! I just need to know that you
value me and are genuinely interested in what goes on inside of me."

Emotional intimacy in a marriage occurs when the needs and desires
of our spouse become as important to us as our own. Furthermore, as
Jane was beginning to understand, our success at that task is not based

on the amount of time we dedicate to it. It is something that occurs over time, through the small interactions we have with each other that show our genuine interest in knowing more about our spouse. It is a journey that takes work, and two open hearts.

Talking Together

What are some of your partner's behaviors that make you feel special in his or her eyes? What are some of the little things you could each do that would show your genuine interest in knowing more about your partner?

Praying Together

Father God, we long to be known by someone, especially by someone we love. Yet we are also afraid to be known—we fear rejection, criticism or judgment. We thank You for knowing us and accepting us. Help us to find that same intimacy in our marriage relationship, as we show each other acceptance and a sense of being valued.
Amen.

DAY 5

We Can Also Enjoy Social Intimacy

And let us not neglect our meeting together, as some people do,
but encourage and warn each other, especially now that the day
of his coming back again is drawing near.

HEBREWS 10:25

I'm a reluctant socializer. There's a part of me that always seems to resist getting into social situations, even with Jan there to break the ice. The strange part of this is that, over the years, I have learned that once I'm in a social situation, I can really enjoy myself. Yet my reluctance has never been cured.

Some tests show that about a fourth of our population is introverted. And it isn't just men who are the reluctant socializers—just as many women are that way also. Many of us are drained of energy by social interaction, and when that happens we long for some solitude so that we can recharge our batteries.

This, however, means that most of the population is energized by social situations. They are drained of energy if they are cut off from people. For many of these people, it is relaxing to be in a social situation. Jan is that way.

We're like a lot of couples—opposites do seem to attract. For years, Jan took my reluctance to socialize as something that was wrong with me. It sometimes even felt to her like I didn't want to be with her, that I was rejecting her in some way. Now she knows and accepts that it is the way I am wired. She has learned not to take it personally.

In the same way, during the early years of our marriage, I could not understand Jan's need to be with people. I found myself thinking, "Aren't I enough for her?" I have had to learn that she is not pressuring me to do it all with her, but that she just needs more people contact than I do.

Very few couples find that they like the same intensity of social interaction. Whether you and your spouse are more alike, or very different in your need for other people, finding a middle ground will require some adjustment, for our natural tendency with innate behaviors like these is to think that somehow our partner should need and want exactly what we need and want. Once we understand and accept our differences, we can have fun building social intimacy together.

Talking Together

Discuss who's the reluctant socializer in your marriage, or at least, who tends to be that way. Who's more social? Has this caused any problems in the past? How can you better coordinate your social life together to satisfy each other's needs?

Praying Together

Father, we are grateful that You want us to enjoy not only our private life together but also our social life. Our marriage is so important to You, and we thank You for caring about even the little things we do that help to strengthen our marriage. Help us to value this part of our intimacy. Where we are out of balance with each other, give us grace and understanding.
Amen.

DAY 6

The Intimacy of Work

*Greet Priscilla and Aquila. They have been co-workers in my ministry
for Christ Jesus. In fact, they risked their lives for me. I am not the only one
who is thankful to them; so are all the Gentile churches.*

ROMANS 16:3-4

What a couple they must have been, this Priscilla and Aquila. In three different letters Paul sends his greetings to them and compliments them on their work together for the ministry. How fascinating it would have been to have sat with them and talked for a couple of hours. They must have had a good marriage, and they certainly must have enjoyed the intimacy shared as they worked together.

You've probably had times when you and your partner have had a big task to do together, and even though it may not have gone smoothly all the time you were working, there was likely a wonderful sense of togetherness and satisfaction when the task was finished.

Recently a couple who were in business together told me, "We really do work together well, but we don't do marriage very well." As we talked together, it became very clear what they meant. While they were at work, they got along great. They could almost finish each other's sentences regarding the store they owned and ran. Yet when they were away from their work, they could still talk only business. There weren't a whole lot of other things going on in their relationship. Their wheel of intimacy was out of balance, and had been for a number of years.

What they were experiencing was very predictable. They had spent hours upon hours together, building their business. During that building time, they were consumed by their work. As the business grew, it demanded even more time and attention in order to succeed. Very little time was left for them to work on the other areas of intimacy. Even the physical side of their relationship was put on the back burner, and part of their concern was that they wanted to work on the relational side of their marriage.

How do they begin? To start with, they need to recognize that they do have one area of intimacy that is very strong. They just need to begin to carve out the time and make the same kind of effort they gave to the development of their business to rediscover in each other the other facets of intimacy.

Talking Together

How well do you work together as a couple? What are the intimacy strengths in your marriage? What areas of intimacy have been more difficult to develop? What are some steps you could begin to take to bring more balance in your marriage?

Praying Together

Dear God, we really want balance in our marriage. We want to be able to enjoy each other in many different ways. We need help with our ability to work together. We want the same kind of enjoyment in working together as we have in other areas of our marriage. We also want to enjoy You more. Help us to always be aware of ways we can increase our enjoyment of each other, for we know You delight in us as individuals and as a couple.
Amen.

DAY 7

Intimacy Is Spelled T-I-M-E

*A newly married man must not be drafted into the army or given any
other special responsibilities. He must be free to be at home for one year,
bringing happiness to the wife he has married.*
DEUTERONOMY 24:5

What an incredible idea! God knows that intimacy takes time, so in
giving the Law, he said that newly married husbands were not to do
anything extra during the first year of marriage so that they could
give themselves completely to their wives. Nothing more is said, either
in the verses before or in the verses after, but so much is said in that
one verse: intimacy between a husband and wife is a priority to God,
and He knows intimacy takes time.

Although this verse speaks of only the first year of marriage, it is
not stretching a point to suggest that couples need to continue to
carve out time for each other, in order to focus on their partner's happiness. Steve and Courtney were a typical suburban couple. Their lives
were ruled by their work and by the demands of their children's schedules. I asked them when they ever found time for just the two of them.

"Well, that's something we hope to find later on, after the kids
are grown up some more," Steve reported. Courtney jumped in and
added, "I'm on the run from the moment I get home—my schedule as
a teacher isn't much different than that of my kids. One is in ballet
three times a week; the other is in speech therapy and is on the Junior
High basketball team. In addition, there is homework every night and
church youth activities two different nights a week. Steve goes to night
school one night a week, and I often have something at the school or
the church one or two nights a month. On the weekend, there's soccer—and oh, I forgot—there's soccer practice one or two nights a week.

Then there's church, and we at least try to have a family night on Sundays, but we don't often get that in. When are we supposed to have time just for ourselves?"

When we have children, much of our time is regulated by their activities. It's not that Steve and Courtney are pushing their kids to do all those things—their kids really want to do them. Yet somehow we must find time for our marriage relationship. It has to be our priority. Our children are important, but the best gift we can give to our children is for us to be "marriage centered." To be marriage centered means we take time to be with each other—alone!

Talking Together

It is difficult to balance everything that's required for our work schedules and for our children, and what is required to guard our marital relationship. How would you describe the balance you have between children, work and your marriage? Talk about what change you could begin to make to carve out more time for just the two of you.

Praying Together

Dear Lord, we would like to have more time to focus on our marriage relationship. Yet, we can't seem to make it happen. Maybe there is some fear inside of us that causes us to back away from what we really want. Help us to get control of our schedule so that we can move more toward each other and be able not only to spend time together but to also grow closer to each other and to You.

Amen.

RESOLVING CONFLICTS

DAY 1

Conflict Is Not Terminal

Get rid of all bitterness, rage, anger, harsh words, and slander, as well as all types
of malicious behavior. Instead, be kind to each other, tenderhearted, forgiving one
another, just as God through Christ has forgiven you.

EPHESIANS 4:31-32

Conflict is a part of a healthy marriage. Researchers have found that many couples who never fight eventually leave the marriage, because they have become strangers. Other couples fight all the time because that's the only way they know how to relate to each other.

One couple who fought constantly came to my office, seeking counseling. I suggested a way for them to limit their arguments to a specific twenty-minute period each day. They thought that would be impossible, but they were willing to give it a try. After a week, they reported that they could hardly fill the twenty minutes with conflict issues, but that they felt things had gotten worse between them. The conflicts had almost disappeared, and now they were confronted with finding new ways to relate to each other.

I had asked them to use the twenty minutes in the following way. Each was to get ten minutes to talk. While one talked, his or her partner was to take copious notes on what he or she was saying. The reason they were to take notes was that they could not respond that night to anything that was said—they had to wait twenty-four hours to respond. Obviously, this couple had a new experience together of listening to what was being said. Once they felt heard, they found there was no need to keep the argument alive.

It's not whether you have conflict in your marriage that determines success or failure, but rather how you behave when you have a conflict. Paul urges the Ephesians to "Get rid of all bitterness, rage, anger, harsh words, and slander, as well as all types of malicious behavior." That's a tall order! We know we can't completely rid ourselves of those behaviors, but we can at least limit them in our lives. Paul continues on to say we are to "be kind to each other, tenderhearted, forgiving one another, just as God through Christ has forgiven you." The question is not "Do we have conflict?" but rather, "How do we behave when we have conflict?" Couples who succeed in marriage have learned how to disagree and how to hold on to their spouse at the same time.

Talk Together

Discuss how you as a couple handle potential conflict situations. Are there parts of the pattern you'd like to change? What are some ways you could help each other behave as Paul urges us to behave when faced with a conflict situation?

Pray Together

*Father, help us to understand that conflicts always come when
two people come together. We struggle with being one, yet still being
ourselves. Help us to remember to be kind in the midst of a conflict,
and with Your help to always remember that whatever is going
on between us is not going to be terminal.*
Amen.

DAY 2

Holding On in the Conflict

So be careful how you live, not as fools but as those who are wise.
Make the most of every opportunity for doing good in these evil days. Don't act
thoughtlessly, but try to understand what the Lord wants you to do.
EPHESIANS 5:15-17

How does one hold on to another person in the midst of a conflict? Emotions are running high; the other person isn't listening; you're becoming increasingly frustrated—at that point it's easy to disengage and not really care anymore. You can see how easy it would be to let go of the other person when you feel like you've reached the end of your rope and you're barely able to hold on.

Sally described how she let go of her husband. She had had it with Dick and his constant arguing with everything she said. "That's it! I'm seeing the lawyer today," she had yelled. "You say you were happier before we married, so now you can be happy again. I'll have my things packed and I will be gone by the time you get home!" And with that, she had stormed out of the house. Now, she was wondering how she could back off from her declaration. If she withdrew her threat, would Dick ever take her seriously in the future? If she followed through on her threat, she would be forced to do something she didn't really want to do. She had forgotten to "hold on to the other person" in the midst of the conflict.

Paul urges us to be "careful how you live" and to live "as those who are wise." Yet we all know how easy it is to "act thoughtlessly" when we have been overwhelmed by frustration, hurt and anger. Paul understands the difficulty of what he is saying, for he finishes this thought with the words "but try . . ." It's a growth process. We can't just automatically will ourselves to be careful when our emotions are on a rampage. We have to work at it and "try to understand what the Lord wants you to do."

The presence of conflict in our marriages isn't the problem—it's what we do once we have entered into the conflict. How do we repair the hurting words? How do we fix something that has escalated beyond what we know to be wise? Paul says, "Try to understand." Yes, understand what the Lord wants you to do, but also try to understand what's going on inside your partner. Show your desire to understand through a gentle touch, an impromptu "I love you," or a steady gaze that communicates a desire to listen.

Talk Together

Talk together about some times when you have had a conflict and been able to "hold on to each other" during the conflict. What do you think made that possible?

Pray Together

Father, we don't always try to understand each other, let alone try to understand what You want us to do in a situation. Help us to be more aware of what our partner is experiencing when we have a conflict. Help us to learn how to communicate our love for each other even when we aren't feeling very loving.

Amen.

DAY 3

Conflict Is No Excuse for Rudeness

We all make many mistakes, but those who control their tongues can also control themselves in every other way.

JAMES 3:2

In one of our seminars we talk about some of the negative behaviors couples do that can erode the strength of their marriage. One of these behaviors in called "contemptuousness," which is a giant step beyond criticism. With this type of behavior, which usually occurs in a conflict that has escalated out of control, one person begins to attack the character of the other person. Name calling, sarcastic humor, statements indicating disgust—all are part of contempt. We also talked about the more subtle behaviors that communicate contempt, and one very prominent behavior is "the eye roll." When people show contempt in this way, they usually roll their eyes up and to the right, and form sort of a sneering look with their mouth.

At the break, a couple came up to us to talk about contemptuous behavior. The wife said that in her family it was a very common behavior for people to roll their eyes like that as the family members talked animatedly around the table. "It really doesn't mean anything negative to me," she said. "I just do it as part of my animated response to my husband."

We looked over at her husband, who was standing next to her. He looked like he had a different opinion. I asked him, "How does it feel to you when she rolls her eyes like that when you are talking together?"

"It feels just like you say—it's very negative and hurtful. I feel like she is not only dismissing what I am saying but also dismissing me."

"But I'm not," she quickly responded. "It doesn't have any of that meaning for me!"

"Yet it does for him," I pointed out, "and that is what you have to go by. You may not mean anything by it because you have become immune to its effect through your family experience, but that's not his experience. You have to go by how he receives that behavior." What had become meaningless to her still had great meaning to him, and that was what was important—it's how the message is received that counts.

That's true about a lot of our behaviors, especially when we are in a conflict. We need to be careful to pay attention to how our words and our actions are experienced by our partner.

Talking Together

All of us lose it at some time for, as James says, the tongue is tough to control. Talk about what contemptuousness means to you. Think of a situation when you've seen someone act contemptuously with someone else. What do you think caused him or her to lose control? Has this ever happened in your marriage?

Praying Together

Father, we know how hard it is to control our tongues, especially when we are upset. You know we love each other and don't want to hurt each other, so we ask You to help us at those times when our emotions are strong and our tongues are loose. May we bring honor to You and to each other in the way we treat each other.
Amen.

DAY 4

Conflict Can Be a Facet of Intimacy

As iron sharpens iron, a friend sharpens a friend.
PROVERBS 27:17

The intimacy we can share in conflict can be summed up in the state-ment often heard that, "yes, the fights are rough, but it's the making up afterward that is great!" While we can agree with this saying's en-thusiasm, none of us would say that we enjoy conflict, or that we cre-ate conflict so that we can enjoy making up afterward. Yet, conflict need not be a negative part of married life.

Researchers say that it takes eight to twelve years for a couple to settle in with each other. During that time there are a number of ad-justments that need to be made. Some couples are more flexible and the adjustments are easier; other couples may have control issues—like Jan and I did—and struggle through this period.

Conflict can either tear us apart or build a greater intimacy in the relationship. Couples who are afraid of conflict or who do not know how to keep the conflict from escalating out of control not only are in great danger in their marriages but also miss out on the intimacy lessons contained in the conflict. It's as if the sparks that come from the "iron sharpening iron" type of conflict instead set off sparks that ignite a forest fire.

These are the couples that haven't found out how to harness the conflict and keep it within the parameters of safety. As the conflict escalates, they say things that wound deeply. Furthermore, they don't know how to make up afterward and repair the hurt feelings experi-enced during the conflict. Instead of making up, they go into silent periods that often last for a week or more. That kind of conflict needs to be avoided!

Bill and Laura used to experience arguments that led to silence that would go on for days. "We got scared," Bill said, "and we got help. We had to learn how to slow down and listen. That made all the difference for us—that and remembering that we really did love each other. Once we put those principles into practice, our times of conflict became times of building greater closeness in our relationship."

When we learn how to contain our conflicts, rather than avoiding them or overreacting, we build strength of character within each of us, and we build another part of the intimacy cycle that strengthens our marriage relationship.

Talking Together

On a scale from avoiding conflict to overreacting to conflict, where would you place your typical behavior? Since we want to avoid both extremes on this scale, what can you do, or what do you already do, to keep your conflict situations manageable? Talk about a time when it was especially nice to "make up."

Praying Together

Lord, You know our hearts. We are grateful for Your enjoyment of us as a couple. We know You sometimes wonder about how we approach or even avoid conflict with each other. Help us to be more comfortable with our conflicts. Give us grace for those situations that never seem to go away. Help us not to take ourselves so seriously that we lose sight of each other and of You.

Amen.

DAY 5

Conflict Is to Be Kept Short

And "don't sin by letting anger gain control over you." Don't let the sun go down
while you are still angry, for anger gives a mighty foothold to the Devil.
EPHESIANS 4:26-27

I have a cartoon that shows a couple sitting in their marriage counselor's office. The counselor is sitting behind his desk, and the couple is on the other side. The husband has his head on the desk and is fast asleep. The wife is almost asleep, and she says to the counselor, "Of course we're sleepy. We haven't slept all week. You told us not to go to bed angry." Obviously they took the counselor's, and Paul's, words literally.

Perhaps it is better to take Paul literally than to ignore what he is saying here. Dan and Esther ignored Paul's advice. I hadn't seen them for two weeks when they came in for their session. Esther started by saying, "We haven't talked to each other since we were here last time. We had an argument on the way home, and neither one of us has spoken since." Dan cynically disagreed as he pointed out that several times he had spoken—he had asked about whether a meal was going to be made or not.

It always amazes me that so many couples give each other the silent treatment—in this case for two weeks. Not only is that a cruel, punishing behavior in a marriage, but, as Paul points out, it gives "a mighty foothold to the Devil." In our silence we are nursing our grudges and our resentments. At the same time, we are allowing feelings of contempt and disrespect for our partners to grow.

This attitude of disrespect for our partners is counter to what Scripture is clearly calling us to do. Not only are we to respect our parents (see Lev. 19:3) and the elderly (see Lev. 19:32), we are also called as an act of obedience to respect our marriage partners. Peter tells husbands especially to "give honor to your wives" (1 Pet. 3:7). In fact, Peter calls us as believers to "show respect for everyone" (1 Pet. 2:17).

Resentments set off a vicious cycle in our thoughts that grows over time. In the same way, an attitude of respect for others sets off a peaceful cycle in our thoughts that also grows over time. Perhaps the hardest place to show continued respect for another person is in our marriages. Yet this is probably the most important place for us to practice that respect.

Talking Together

Everyone wants to be respected. Talk together about the areas where you really feel your partner respects you. What makes you feel his or her respect? In what ways might anger be related to feelings of disrespect?

Praying Together

Lord, we acknowledge that each of us desires to be respected, especially by our partner. We thank You for those areas in our marriage where we do show that respect to each other. Perhaps there are areas where we need to experience more respect, or to give more respect, where one of us may be experiencing hurt, anger and disappointment. Help us in those areas of our marriage to grow stronger so as not to give the devil any foothold in our relationship.
Amen.

DAY 6

Conflict Requires Repairs

Think of ways to encourage one another to outbursts of love and good deeds.
HEBREWS 10:24

We had a conflict recently that illustrated how we can make repairs in our relationship quickly afterward. Jan was picking up some gifts at the shopping center and I was waiting in the car for her. She had put the gifts on hold, thinking that I had the checkbook, and she had come running back to the car to ask me for it. Instead, she realized she had had the checkbook all along, and rushed back to the store to pay for the items.

When she came back with the bag containing the gift items, it seemed awfully heavy to me, so I asked her, "How many did you buy?" I didn't realize how Jan heard my comment until she said, "Why do you always have to say something like that? You always question what I do." As I tried to backtrack and explain myself, it just got worse. I said with a pout, "Then I just won't ask you any more questions." Then, like a typical male, I stopped talking for a while.

Later that night I made a strange attempt to repair the situation. I asked Jan a question: "Are you sorry that you misunderstood me?" My absurd question struck a funny bone in Jan and she started laughing, and soon I was laughing, too, at the ridiculousness of what I had asked. As we talked about my question, she did apologize and so did I. What we had just done was repair the conflict after the sun had gone down, but before we went to bed and before our time to pray together.

The ability to repair conflicts is what couples whose marriages are lasting have learned. We repair the situation by somehow, in some way, reaching out to our partners. It often includes touch—I know I was reaching out and touching Jan as I asked my question. Any behavior that moves us toward the other person is an invitation to repair any damage that was done in the conflict. Usually these moves are tentative, but they are a clear invitation to fix things.

Of course, what we want to practice are those "outbursts of love and good deeds" that will encourage our partner and pull us closer together. Yet, when we fail in that task, we can develop little ways to repair the situation and get us back on track with each other.

Talking Together

Discuss some of the ways you could make a move toward each other at the end of a conflict. Then talk about how you could do that even in the middle of a conflict. What are some of the ways you already do this?

Praying Together

Dear Lord, You know how much we dislike conflict, but we also recognize that within the struggles of our conflicts lie the seeds of growth and maturing love. Help us to more quickly recognize ways to stop the cycle of conflict once it begins, and to have the courage to reach out in an attempt to repair the situation. Help us to keep our love for each other before us, so that we may more consistently see our partner with the eyes of love.

Amen.

DAY 7

Conflict Provides a Place for Growth

We can rejoice, too, when we run into problems and trials,
for we know that they are good for us—they help us learn to endure.
And endurance develops strength of character in us.
ROMANS 5:3-4

What makes conflict an opportunity for growth? In my years of observing couples in the midst of conflict, I have discovered that those who seem to experience growth are those who keep the tension of the conflict focused on themselves. They somehow keep what is going on between them a guarded piece of information.

Now it is important not to interpret this as advice to keep the conflict a secret, and to suffer in silence. Yet the wise couple is careful about whom they share their problems with. Keith and Joanna were not very wise—at least Joanna wasn't. They were in their first year of marriage and it was a rocky beginning for both of them. Yet Joanna seemed to be especially shaken by their problems. She tried to talk to Keith, but he didn't seem to understand why she was so upset—the problems were there, but they didn't seem that huge to him.

Keith and Joanna had met as youth sponsors in their church, and had looked forward to working with the high school group together after they were married. Joanna shared some of their problems with the youth minister, who wasn't very discreet about the information. That didn't seem to matter, for Joanna seemed to be talking to anyone who listened about what was going on. As others got involved in Keith and Joanna's problems, the problems seemed to grow, and by the time word of them reached the senior pastor, he advised the minister of youth to ask Keith and Joanna to step down from ministry.

Now both of them were humiliated by what had happened. Joanna didn't intend for things to get out of hand, but she had felt that she needed to express her anxiety and hurt somewhere. When she did, however, she found that it didn't really help, for the problem was still there. The more Joanna talked with others about her problem, the less opportunity she found to grow through the problem.

By the time Keith and Joanna got some counseling help, their problems had compounded and they were faced with some really hard work to put things back together. One thing they learned in the process was to be careful about whom they shared things with. Problems were a part of learning to live and grow together. Keith also learned a hard lesson about taking his wife's concerns seriously.

Talking Together

If you had a problem, who would you trust, knowing they could keep a confidence? Talk together about how each of you feels about how conflict can produce growth.

Praying Together

Father God, we need to talk with other people about our lives.
We love being able to talk with You, but we also know that You have
gifted wise counselors who are in tune with Your perspective.
Help us to be wise in our choice of counselors and friends, and help
us to learn how to listen to Your Word so that we have a good
plumb line with which to compare what others say.
Amen.

MAINTAINING FAITHFULNESS

DAY 1

Faithfulness Is Persevering Together

May the Lord direct your hearts into God's love and Christ's perseverance.
2 THESSALONIANS 3:5, *NIV*

Perseverance is a word we typically apply to our faith and our walk with the Lord. It involves the idea of tenacity—of hanging in there. It has a very positive connotation when we think of "persevering in our faith." Yet it takes on a somewhat negative character when we think of "persevering in our marriage." This sounds like an unpleasant type of "hanging in there." Think instead of how that phrase might affect us if we were to ascribe very positive meanings to it in reference to our marriages.

Alice struggled with persevering. She had become emotionally involved with a man from church—nothing physical, just lots of phone conversations and lunches together. Fortunately, it stopped at that level. Yet her husband, Fred, was just as devastated as if it had been a full-blown physical affair. His reaction was to withdraw into silence and hurt. If he spoke at all to Alice, it was with a strong undercurrent of anger in his voice. Finally, Fred suggested that they talk to the pastor, and Alice agreed.

The session with the pastor was quite animated. Fred tried to talk about his hurt, but since it had been three years since the relationship had stopped, Alice let loose with her anger at the fact that Fred was "nursing his pain too long." Fred even admitted that he had been nursing it too long and said that this was why he suggested they come talk to the pastor.

Finally, after things were calmed down, Alice said in a voice of resignation, "I know what I did was wrong, but I just can't handle Fred's anger and silence. I don't know what to do anymore—everything I do is a cause for him to be angry with me." Alice had talked of her frustration a number of times, and each time, Fred had softened. He was caught between his feelings of hurt and his fear of hurting Alice. Yet they had both made a choice—they were persevering, just barely "hanging in there." It was working, for Fred and Alice were at a crossroads, and their choice to persevere would eventually see them through this tough period.

Perseverance is a positive discipline that carries us through the very difficult times, like those Fred and Alice were experiencing. In a marriage, we need to think of persevering as "holding on to each other." It's acting on the principle that no matter how difficult an issue might be, we're holding on to our relationship and to each other.

Talking Together

Perseverance is an attitude that means we hold on to the other. In what ways do you "hold on" to each other? Can you think of some additional ways you might communicate your commitment—your "hanging in there" with each other?

Praying Together

Father in heaven, we are committed to each other and we are grateful for our marriage. Yet there are times when we get so discouraged, or so hassled by life, that we feel like giving up. Give us added strength and wisdom at those times. You've promised to give us wisdom when we ask, and we ask for that in relation to our marriage. Thank You for Your faithfulness to us.
Amen.

DAY 2

Faithfulness Is Different from Happiness

So guard yourself, remain loyal to the wife of your youth.
MALACHI 2:15

It seems like everyone in this day and age is interested in happiness. If someone makes us feel happy, we want to be with him or her. We may even want to marry that person, and do so only to find out that eventually he or she can now make us feel unhappy. Most couples divorce in the fifth year of marriage, and the most common reason given to me as a counselor is, "I deserve to be happy, and I'm not happy in this marriage. So I'm getting out."

Ben said this to me after finding out that his wife had had lunch with an old flame. He felt betrayed by her behavior and in his hurt he felt like everything in their short marriage had been bad. Nothing was going to change his mind, and that weekend he moved out. Nothing I said mattered, and nothing his wife said to him made any difference—he was finished.

One of the points I shared with Ben concerned the results of a recent study of couples that reported themselves as being very unhappy in their lives and in their marriages. The researchers followed up five years later on those couples that had stayed married. Without exception, they reported that they were now happy with life and happy in their marriages. Those who had divorced because they were unhappy reported that they were still unhappy. I thought this was pretty amazing, but Ben wasn't listening. He'd already made up his mind and was going to continue his search for happiness apart from his wife.

Couples who have been married for a long time really aren't too amazed at the results of that study. They know that marriages go through highs and lows of happiness and dissatisfaction. They also know the value of being faithful to their vows and working things through together.

It is a foolish person who seeks to discover happiness in life, or in his or her marriage. It's not that we don't want to experience happiness together; the foolishness is in seeking after happiness. Happiness is always a by-product of something else. If we seek it directly, happiness will elude us. If we seek after godliness, and faithfulness to our partner, happiness will find us.

Be careful what you seek after, for God has clearly given us the guidelines to experiencing true happiness.

Talking Together

Look back over your relationship. In what situations have you experienced happiness? What caused you to feel happy together? What are some of the other things you do, or have done, that bring a sense of joy and happiness to you both?

Praying Together

Almighty God, help us to avoid the maddening search for happiness that seems to consume so many people we know. Help us to experience the deep joy that comes from seeking after You— especially when we seek You together. May the joy and happiness we experience with You be contagious to those we love.
Amen.

DAY 3

Faithfulness Is to Be Our Goal

But Jesus told him, "Anyone who puts a hand to the plow and then
looks back is not fit for the Kingdom of God."

LUKE 9:62

Jesus' words recorded in Luke 9 are addressed to a would-be disciple who tried to beg off in following Jesus in order to first say good-bye to his family. Jesus was describing the cost of following after Him. I think His words are just as appropriate for us in the context of marriage. After all, our marriages are a part of our discipleship, and we've already noted how interested God is in our marriages. So we can take the principle in verse 62 and paraphrase it to say, "Anyone who gives his vow to God and his or her partner and then looks back and wants to renege on it is not fit for the kingdom of God."

Wow, that's what discipleship is all about as a couple—faithfulness over the years. Yet what about those who have looked back at some point and then after the divorce have remarried? Start where you are today and build faithfulness into your marriage now to last for a lifetime.

Carl and Frieda were concerned about this. Frieda had been married before and was just now dealing with the spiritual issues related to her divorce. As she struggled with the past, she was also wreaking havoc with her present situation. While it was helpful that she was dealing with the issues from her past, she had to be careful not to let this jeopardize her current marriage. "I know there was nothing more I could have done in that marriage," Frieda said. "He left me for his secretary, but I still feel guilty about it, like there was something I could have done differently that would have saved the marriage."

I agreed with her struggle and said that there appeared to be things from the past with which she needed to deal. Yet I added, "You need to see the issue of faithfulness in your current situation as the priority. God has called you to be faithful in the here and now. This is the relationship that counts." I then went on to point out how, in the passage quoted previously, Jesus is calling people to follow after Him and they are delaying their commitment to discipleship with excuses in the here and now.

We all have things in our past that call into question our faithfulness to God and to those we love. It may be anything that we have experienced in our past that we regret. While we need to repent of those things and accept God's forgiveness, we also need to see faithfulness as a calling that begins right here and right now.

Talking Together

Talk about how people see the call to discipleship today. What excuses have you heard? How does the call to faithfulness do away with the excuses? How does the call to discipleship impact your marriage?

Praying Together

Heavenly Father, we want to be faithful disciples of Yours,
both individually and as a couple. Help us to discern what excuses
we may hold on to that keep us from being Your fully committed
followers. Help us to see what resentments we hold on to as a couple
that keep our marriage from reflecting that commitment.
Amen.

DAY 4

Faithfulness Carries Us Through the Dark Times

But now, call Israel to account, for she is no longer my wife,
and I am no longer her husband.

HOSEA 2:2

God's relationship with Israel had been rocky, to say the least. There were times of great joy, such as when Solomon dedicated the temple. Yet there were also times of anger, hurt and frustration, as when Israel rejected God and chose to worship idols. As a result of Israel's unfaithfulness, God allowed foreign kings to conquer the Israelites, and even carry them off into captivity. Then there was that long period of silence that covered the more than four hundred years from the closing of the Old Testament until the coming of Jesus.

As we read over the paragraph regarding Israel and her relationship with God, it might remind us of the relational description of most marriages. We go through times of great joy, times of hurt and frustration, and times of silence. There are also the dark times every marriage seems to experience. We experienced the dark times when one of our kids got involved in the drug culture. For a number of years, we often didn't know whether he was alive or dead. Fortunately, with God's grace, he survived and now has many years of living in recovery, but those were very dark years for us.

One of the things we held on to during those years was the faithfulness of God. It wasn't easy, for there were times when we had arranged situations and circumstances to help God perform a miracle, yet nothing happened and we struggled together with what God's part was to be in our painful situation.

After what seemed like a long period of silence on God's part, suddenly things started to happen that were completely out of our control. God was faithful—He was acting, and all we could do was stand by, watch and rejoice! Looking back, we can see that even in the darkest times, we persevered in holding on to the faithfulness of God. We held on to each other as we prayed. We don't know what it would have been like for us had we not already had in place the commitment we made earlier to pray together daily. God sustained us throughout those difficult dark times.

When we go through the dark periods of life, it is important not only that we hold on to the faithfulness of God in those circumstances, but that we stay faithful to each other. We must hold on to each other in the confident assurance that God is present and that He cares.

Talking Together

Everyone's dark period is different. Sometimes, when we compare our difficult time with someone else's, ours seems to pale in comparison, but ours is what we experienced. Talk over some of the times of darkness you have personally experienced in your life. How did you hold on to God?

Praying Together

Lord Jesus, we are grateful that You are faithful. You came to earth to die for our sins, and You were faithful in that ultimate task. You are called faithful and true in the Scriptures, and we want that to be our testimony. Help us to be faithful, not only to You but also to each other, regardless of the circumstances of our lives.

Amen.

DAY 5

Faithfulness Can Be Broken and Repaired

Go and get your wife again. Bring her back to you and love her,
even though she loves adultery. For the Lord still loves Israel even
though the people have turned to other gods.

HOSEA 3:1

The story of Hosea's marriage is remarkable. He was told to marry a woman who was a prostitute, and he did. After they were married, she left him to go back to her work as a prostitute. Hosea's marriage was a picture of God's relationship with Israel. The amazing part is that God told Hosea to go and seek out his wife and restore her and his marriage. He found her and had to buy her back and bring her home. The restoration of his wife Gomer is an incredible picture of how God restores us to Himself.

Will had been unfaithful to his wife seven years before. It had been a short liaison with a co-worker that had ended quickly when Bev found out what was happening. They had wept together for a while and then it had all been put away as if it had been resolved. Now Will was saying that he was not sure he wanted to stay in the marriage. He was overworked, gone a lot, and under a lot of pressure, and said he needed to get away to think. As he talked about all of this, Bev's thoughts kept going back to the incident seven years before.

"It all feels the same to me," she said. "I feel like I'm reliving what happened back then." Will's response was, "You think that way every couple of months. You've never let me forget what happened back then. I've had to walk on eggshells ever since that happened, and I'm tired of it."

Faithfulness had been broken seven years before, but the repairs had never been completed. As a result, that event still lived on in their relationship—faithfulness was still broken. What Will didn't understand was that when faithfulness is broken, it takes time for both people to be able to repair the damage. A quick Band-Aid over the wound isn't going to allow for healing. Bev and Will eventually came to the conclusion that they were now willing to do the work of repair together.

When Hosea brought Gomer home, she lived in the house with Hosea but she also had to prove herself. Everything didn't just go back to "normal" when she got home. Hosea knew that it would take time to heal the wounds caused by her unfaithfulness. Yet the important lesson from Hosea is that faithfulness can be restored.

Talking Together

Every person in a marriage experiences some woundedness at the hands of his or her partner. But the repairs are more important than the wounds. How have you repaired any wounds in your marriage? Talk about any unfinished business you may have with each other in this area.

Praying Together

Father, we know we are imperfect humans and that we are prone to sin. We are grateful that You are a forgiving father. Help us to learn how to better repair the wounds we cause each other. Give us patience, understanding, and an extra measure of grace as we seek to repair the wounds we have experienced.

Amen.

DAY 6

Faithfulness Is a Matter of the Heart

Teach me your ways, O Lord, that I may live according to your truth!
Grant me purity of heart, that I may honor you.
PSALM 86:11

When we make faithfulness a matter of the heart, what we are looking at is a question of loyalty. In Webster's definition of "faithful," it includes the idea of loyalty and reliability, even going so far as to add the descriptive word "constant" to these two terms. Many of the couples with whom I talk are struggling with the question of loyalty and of reliability. In these cases, one partner is usually questioning whether the other person is really there for him or her.

Debra was explaining the hurt she was feeling in her marriage relationship. Al kept trying to interrupt her to defend himself. I asked him to wait, and said that he could give his side of the story in a moment. Debra had heard some of his defenses, probably many times before, so she started to qualify her concerns. "Yes, he does help me sometimes and he does do things around the house. But it's only after I've had to ask him over and over that he will finally tear himself away from what he is watching on TV and help. He's either on the computer or glued to the TV."

When Al began to explain himself, he listed all of the things he did for Debra and for their son. As he finished, he added, "I just don't understand what her problem is. A lot of wives would be happy with what I do."

As I looked back at Debra, she sighed as she said, "I guess it's a question of his loyalty. He talks all the time to his friends and to his co-workers, but he never sits down and talks with me like a friend anymore. Nothing keeps him from his golf appointments. It seems like everything else is far more important to him than I am."

Al had a heart problem. He was helping Debra with tasks, but she never sensed that his heart was there. It was always somewhere else. He worked at home and hadn't learned how to keep office hours separate from family and wife hours. As far as Debra could see, he was always working. He admitted he loved talking with friends, but didn't know how to talk to Debra anymore. She was seeing Al through the eyes of Matthew 6:21: "Wherever your treasure is, there your heart and thoughts will also be." Whether it was Al's intent or not, the message he was giving to Debra was that she was not in first place in his life. Debra wanted his heart more than she wanted his help.

Talking Together

What do you think makes it hard to understand our partner's heart at times? How could you help each other better communicate "heart" concerns? Talk about a time when you felt your heart concerns were understood by your spouse.

Praying Together

Lord, we know that You know our hearts. You know everything about us. Sometimes it is hard for us to let our partners know what we need from them. Help us to have the courage to express our hearts' need—but to also respond more openly to our mates' needs. Give us ears to hear each other's hearts and to respond to what is needed.

Amen.

DAY 7

Faithfulness Is Being Full of Faith

If we are unfaithful, he remains faithful, for he cannot deny himself.
2 TIMOTHY 2:13

Paul gives Timothy a great promise and assurance. He is basically saying that God can never be unfaithful in his relationship with us, for faithfulness is an attribute of his character. Unfortunately, that isn't true for us. Because we are sinful people, we have times when we are unfaithful and disloyal, but we want to minimize those times as best we can. We do that by filling ourselves with faith.

One could define faithful as being "full of faith." I love it when I see a couple that truly believes in each other. I talked with a couple recently with whom I had also met several years ago. When I met with them the first time, they were struggling with their marriage relationship and Lou was not feeling very good about Carol. Carol had done some hurtful things in their marriage, and Lou didn't have much confidence in her anymore. They successfully worked through those concerns and seemed to be on the right track.

This time when I saw them it was related to a work concern for Carol. After she described the situation, Lou jumped in and started to affirm Carol instead of trying to fix her. He told her how proud he was of her, how he believed in her and her abilities. He affirmed her as a mother and as a wife. Then he said, "I have every confidence that Carol can work this out, but we both felt we needed an objective opinion on what to do."

I couldn't help but comment on the changes in his attitude toward Carol, and how wonderful that was. They went on to describe what had happened in between our visits—how they had talked things through, how they had started praying together daily, and how they had made a commitment to each other to communicate regularly about how they believed in their marriage and in each other. They had obviously succeeded, for they were "full of faith" in each other. It was clear that they were not putting on an act. I watched Carol's face as Lou affirmed her, and her eyes sparkled as she listened. Over the preceding years they had built into their marriage the characteristic of faithfulness. They knew what it was to be loyal and faithful to each other.

Talking Together

In what ways do you communicate your "faith" or belief in your partner? Talk about ways you might more often affirm the goodness you see in each other.

Praying Together

Heavenly Father, how we rejoice in Your faithfulness to us. What an assurance to know that, regardless of what we do, You are always going to be faithful, for that is Your nature. We want more of that in our marriage, Lord. We want to not only believe in each other, but also learn how to communicate that "faith" in our partner to him or her.
Amen.

PRAYING TOGETHER

Prayer Is Our Primary Business

Be joyful always; pray continually; give thanks in all circumstances,
for this is God's will for you in Christ Jesus.
1 THESSALONIANS 5:16-18, *NIV*

Slipped into the list of behaviors Paul urges the Thessalonians to express is the little phrase "pray continually." How does one do that? Over the centuries, monks have withdrawn from society to enter into a life of contemplation and prayer. Yet is this the only way one can live out this injunction? I don't think so, for Paul isn't speaking to a select group of people; he's addressing the whole church at Thessalonica.

While we may never know exactly what Paul meant for us specifically, it is clear from what he is saying that prayer is at the heart of our relationship with God. We are to constantly be aware of His presence with us, and to always be open to responding to Him. This is as true for a couple as it is for an individual.

I met with a pastor and his wife who were on the verge of disaster in their marriage. He was known as a very devout man and had had a very strong ministry in our area. Yet he had neglected his marriage, and, as a couple, they were in trouble. I asked them if they ever prayed together, just the two of them. They looked at each other, and I could tell by the looks on their faces what they were going to say.

"Yes, we've prayed together as a couple at times in the past when we have faced a crisis," the wife said, "but neither one of us has ever really been comfortable praying together. Prayer is important in our personal walk with the Lord, but as a couple, we never really think of it."

I was firm with them. I said, "I didn't know that marriage was the exception to our 'Praying constantly.'" I went on to add, "I want you to start praying together every day. You don't have to pray long—I just want you to pray as a couple. I don't think you'll make it in your marriage unless you start praying together now."

They listened to me and began the discipline of praying together. Over the months ahead we were able to work through some very difficult issues that they had avoided all of their married life. I believe it was their praying together that made the difference.

Talking Together

If you already pray together as a couple, talk together about how that has strengthened your marriage. If you haven't been praying together as a couple on a daily basis, talk about what has kept you from praying together. Then make the commitment to begin, even if you agree only to pray silently together.

Praying Together

Father, we want to come into Your presence together as a couple.
We enjoy talking with You individually, but we want to learn
more about how to pray effectively as a couple. Help us to begin
or expand our praying together so that our spiritual intimacy
with You will grow stronger each day.
Amen.

DAY 2

Praying Together Holds Us Accountable

So if you are standing before the altar in the Temple, offering a sacrifice to God,
and you suddenly remember that someone has something against you,
leave your sacrifice there beside the altar. Go and be reconciled to that person.
Then come and offer your sacrifice.
MATTHEW 5:23-24

As we mentioned before, Jan and I have been praying together as a couple for over thirty years. We pray together at night before going to bed. It's always interesting to see what happens when we've had a disagreement that day. If it hasn't been resolved, what are we going to do about praying together?

Sometimes I'm more upset than Jan, so when she comes to bed and asks, "Are we going to pray?" I say, "Nope." Usually she responds by saying, "Well, I am," and she begins to pray. Usually I pray first, but on those nights, she prays first. Of course, I listen, and one of the rules of praying together as a couple is that you never use prayer as a way to preach at your partner. She simply prays.

By the time she finishes, I have softened my own heart and I go ahead and pray as well. When we both finish, we usually apologize for the misunderstanding and work things out together. Praying together has helped us both be accountable to each other before the Lord.

Of course, there are times when the problem between us is bigger and neither one of us offers to pray. We lay there in our proud discomfort and try to sleep, but usually it is a rough night for both of us. By morning, we are ready to leave our "sacrifice there beside the altar" and work on being reconciled. It's time to talk through the issue, which is really easier with the perspective gained by time. Once again, however, it is the discipline of praying together that has held us accountable to each other.

It's interesting that in the passage quoted in today's reading, Jesus is speaking to the one who remembers "that someone has something against you." He is speaking to the offender. As the offender comes to pray, the act of worship and prayer brings to mind the offense and the injunction is to go and make things right. When the offender in the marriage relationship makes the move to make things right, it is a good indicator of a sensitive spirit—one that makes for a good marriage.

Talking Together

We've all had times when the Spirit of God has touched our hearts and held us accountable for something we did that offended. When has this happened to you? What did you do when that happened? How did it impact your marriage?

Praying Together

Father, we want to be sensitive to our partners and to their hurts and needs. We open ourselves to Your Spirit to bring to our minds those times and situations where we need to go and make things right. Give us the courage to be obedient in those situations. We look forward to the blessing You will bring to us as we obey. Amen.

DAY 3

Prayer Is Directly Related to Our Marriage

In the same way, you husbands must give honor to your wives. Treat her
with understanding as you live together. She may be weaker than you are,
but she is your equal partner in God's gift of new life. If you don't treat her
as you should, your prayers will not be heard.

1 PETER 3:7

Peter is clearly linking our effectiveness in our prayer life with how we as husbands are treating our wives. Although he doesn't say it, I would think that the principle is just as true for wives—if you are having trouble with the way you are treating your husband, you'll have trouble in your prayer life. According to the apostle Peter, there is quite obviously a direct link between how we are getting along as a couple and how willing God is to listen to our prayers.

Harry had almost given up on his faith. He told me, "It seems that no matter what I do, God just doesn't hear my prayers." He went on to talk about how others he knew had answers to prayer, and some even talked about the close, intimate relationship they had with the Lord. "I've never felt that. I guess I'm just a second-class Christian. God's apparently not interested in me."

We weren't meeting to work on his marriage, but to work on the feelings of anxiety and panic that intruded into his life at inopportune times. Yet, thinking about what Peter had said, I began to ask him about his relationship with his wife.

"Oh, we just put up with each other," Harry reported. "We don't have a very close relationship. I'm often angry with her, for it seems to me that she is always discounting me and what I say. Nothing I tell her ever seems to matter to her. She pretty much operates as a single woman."

Harry had been married more than thirty years, and as we talked about his marriage, he added some important facts about their relationship. "We haven't had sex together in over a year, probably. We just stay married because neither one of us believes in divorce."

As we talked, Harry told me about other problems they ignored in their marriage relationship. I suggested to him that maybe the reason God didn't seem to answer his prayers was that he needed to make some major repairs in his marital relationship. It was clear that neither of them was treating the other the way a married couple should, and, as Peter makes clear, that blocks the effectiveness of our prayers.

Talking Together

Have you ever had the experience of feeling like your prayers have hit the ceiling and bounced back because of the way you were treating each other? In contrast, what do you experience in your praying when you and your partner are really "in sync" with each other?

Praying Together

Lord God, we want to be effective in our prayer, and we want to be loving and open in our marriage relationship. Help us to see the connection between our treatment of each other and our effectiveness with and openness to You. Keep us from the hypocrisy that says everything is okay in our relationship with You when we are having problems with each other.

Amen.

DAY 4

Our Prayer Life Is Related to Our Sex Life

So do not deprive each other of sexual relations. The only exception to this rule would be the agreement of both husband and wife to refrain from sexual intimacy for a limited time, so they can give themselves more completely to prayer.

1 CORINTHIANS 7:5

When we wrote the book *When Couples Pray Together*, we did a survey of over several hundred couples who had committed to pray together daily for six weeks and were willing to give us a report. Many of their responses to the survey are reported in that book. We learned a lot from what these couples shared with us, and there were some great testimonies of what God had done as they followed through and prayed together daily.

A number of couples commented on the surprising fact that when they were praying together daily, their sexual relationship markedly improved. They said this as an aside, almost not sure what the connection was. We were sharing this with a small couples group, and one couple who had been involved in a university campus ministry said, "Oh, yes. We've always been told that prayer stimulates the same part of the brain as sex. That's why we were always told to counsel unmarried couples to not begin praying together until they were married."

I haven't found any factual research to support this statement, but I do know what many of our couples reported. My guess would be that when a couple develops spiritual intimacy, this results in a very powerful sense of togetherness, and the intimacy shared could very easily lead to a desire for physical intimacy. I do know that no one coached those who responded to our survey to say what they did, and apparently the improvement was great enough to be noticed by those who commented on it.

I'm not sure that Paul had this in mind when he wrote his first letter to the Corinthians, but he does connect sexual relations between a husband and a wife with prayer. Both are a form of communication and the better we communicate as a couple, the richer our experience will be with each other. That's true physically, emotionally and spiritually.

Talking Together

In what ways do you see a couple's sexual relationship as a form of communication? How do you think prayer, which is communicating with God, affects your communication with each other?

Praying Together

Lord, You have given us many gifts, but the gift of prayer and the gift of sex are very important to us. It may seem like we give different priorities to these two gifts, but we want to be in agreement on this. Help us to hear and understand each other better. Keep us from assuming we know what our partner feels regarding sex and prayer. We long for hearts that can really hear each other. Amen.

DAY 5

Prayer Is Sharing Our Hearts

*And this is my prayer: that your love may abound more and more in
knowledge and depth of insight, so that you may be able to discern what is
best and may be pure and blameless until the day of Christ.*
PHILIPPIANS 1:9-10, *NIV*

One of the ways we can pray for each other is to pray some of the
prayers of Scripture. The one from Philippians is our favorite—we
pray it for each other, and we pray it for the couples that attend our
workshops. What married couple doesn't want to share in the fruit of
that prayer?

One of the joys of praying together out loud is that we get to hear
our partner's heart. Roberta shared with us some of the things she
and Mac were experiencing as they started to pray together daily.
"We've been married for twenty-six years and I've never known Mac's
heart like I do now that we are praying together." She went on to say
that, "whenever Mac prays for us, for our kids, or for some problem at
work, I get to know him better. I hear his heart as he prays in a way
that I never was able to hear before."

Mac spoke up and agreed, adding, "I don't feel like Roberta is
being intrusive in any way. It seems so natural that I wonder what
kept us from doing this years ago." He went on, "I think that when
Roberta tried to get me to talk about these things, I really didn't
know how to talk. Maybe I was just afraid to open up to her. But with
praying, it's different. I feel like I'm really talking to God and I don't
mind that she listens."

I know that my resistance to praying together in the early years of
our marriage was caused in part by my fear of Jan knowing parts of
me that I wasn't ready to share. I thought I would have to share deep,

dark secrets as we prayed, and that was scary to me. Yet when we finally started to pray together, I found that we didn't have to do that deep, vulnerable type of prayer—we just needed to talk with God together. As we did, we were able to hear each other's hearts in a way that we couldn't really experience any other way.

The key to sharing hearts in prayer is to just pray. Don't fret about how you do it. Just start in a nonthreatening way. It is so important to be intentional about our praying together. One of the things couples who were praying together all agreed upon was the need to keep it simple and to keep it short. The idea is to meet with the Lord together.

Talking Together

What has been your experience when you have prayed together? Have you been able to hear your partner's heart better? If it is hard for you to pray together out loud, talk about what makes that difficult. Then decide on a simple, short way to pray together.

Praying Together

Lord, it is a privilege to be able to talk with You as a couple.
Where we still struggle with this, give us courage and perseverance.
Help us to stick with the discipline until it becomes a part of us.
Make Yourself known to us in some special ways. You've
promised to meet with us—help us sense Your presence.
Amen.

DAY 6

Prayer Is Walking Together with God

Toward evening they heard the Lord God walking about in the garden, so they hid
themselves among the trees. The Lord God called to Adam, "Where are you?"
GENESIS 3:8-9

Apparently God came to the garden each evening to spend time with
Adam and Eve. Can you imagine what that must have been like? Here
were Adam and Eve in a perfect environment, and they didn't have to
pray to someone unseen—they got to spend time with God actually
there in all of His splendor. What an awesome experience that must
have been!

We don't know how many days they were able to enjoy this shared
intimacy with God, but it had to be the highlight of their day. Then
they chose to disobey God and eat of the fruit of the tree they had
been told to leave alone, and everything changed. Immediately, they
were filled with fear, which was an emotion they had never felt before.
With the fear came shame and guilt. So on this particular day, when
they heard God come into the garden to meet them and share time
with them, they hid.

Did you ever notice that the God who knows everything asked
Adam, "Where are you?" I'm sure God knew what had happened, and
even knew where they were hiding. Yet God's respect for Adam allowed Adam to make the choice to reveal himself, as well as to tell
God what had taken place.

We know about the consequences of Adam and Eve's behavior.
Women bear children with intense pain and suffering. In addition,
women seek to control their husbands and that is a detriment to their
relationship. Men have to struggle to subdue the earth, and produce
food only by the sweat of their brow. Then Adam and Eve were ex-

pelled from the garden, never to return to that paradise.

Yet there was another consequence, which wasn't mentioned but certainly took place. No longer would Adam and Eve enjoy their evening walks with God, and the shared intimacy they felt with their Creator. However, thanks to the redeeming work of Christ on the cross, we are able to restore to some degree what was lost in the garden. We can as a couple share intimacy with God through praying together. That's our challenge as a redeemed couple!

Talking Together

What do you think it was like for Adam and Eve to walk together with God in the garden? What might have been some of their conversations? How do we restore to some degree that shared intimacy with God through praying together?

Praying Together

Lord God, how we wish we could experience what Adam and Eve experienced with You back in the garden. Yet we are grateful that because of the death and resurrection of Your Son, Jesus, we can come boldly before You through prayer and begin to experience to some degree the joy of our shared intimacy with You. We ask that You make Yourself known to us in special ways in the days ahead.

Amen.

DAY 7

Prayer Is Our Marital Foundation

What is causing the quarrels and fights among you? Isn't it the whole
army of evil desires at war within you? . . . And yet the reason you don't
have what you want is that you don't ask God for it.

JAMES 4:1-2

For many, prayer is a last ditch effort to get what we want, or think we need. Others approach prayer as if they were coming to Santa Claus with a list of desires. James speaks to both of these errors in the opening words of James 4. He goes on to add that even when we do pray, we don't get what we ask for because our whole motive in asking is wrong. Yet James gives us the answer a few verses later when he writes, "When you bow down before the Lord and admit your dependence on him, he will lift you up and give you honor" (v. 10).

How does this provide a foundation for our marriages? Sean and Lisa were a typical young couple who were doing well in their work and making a lot of money. Then the economy slowed down and Sean was laid off from his high-paying position. He got a good severance and felt he could easily find another position. But he soon found out that jobs at the level he was used to were few and far between.

The severance package had run out, the big house had been sold, and Sean still hadn't found work. Oh, there were jobs he could have taken, but they both agreed they were "beneath him." When they came to talk with me, their marriage was filled with tension and arguing. What had been a good relationship when life was good had deteriorated about to the same level to which their financial status had tumbled. Lisa was angry with Sean over his prideful attitude. Sean was defensive about his own behavior, afraid to admit that he was scared, and fearful of the future.

I asked them about their relationship with the Lord—how had they maintained that part of their marriage through all of this? That's when Lisa started to cry. Without even asking what was going on, I suggested they start praying together daily. It took a while for Sean to agree, but he did. After several weeks of praying together, Sean still hadn't found work, but he and Lisa had rediscovered the secure foundation of their marriage relationship. As Sean started praying with Lisa, he found he was humbling himself before the Lord, and I could reassure him that at some point God would lift him up and give him honor.

Talking Together

How many of the old disagreements in your marriage came from the differences in the things you each wanted and expected in life? What we want may be a good thing for us both, but our spouse may not agree with it. Are you open to praying about these disagreements and different desires? In what ways do you think prayer might help resolve such differences?

Praying Together

Father, we want to be in accord with You in terms of our desires in life. You created us to have different personalities and therefore different interests and desires. Yet we know that we can find harmony as we humble ourselves before You in prayer. Help us to grow in this area of our lives and marriage. Help us to more quickly humble ourselves before You.

Amen.

THE HUSBAND'S ROLE

DAY 1

Submission Is Also for Husbands

And further, you will submit to one another out of reverence for Christ.
EPHESIANS 5:21

Submission is a controversial subject for some husbands. They like verse 22 better, which directs the wife to be submissive. Kyle was one who believed in verse 22 and ignored verse 21. He and his wife came in to see me, and I asked them, "What brings you here?" After a moment of silence, Kyle spoke up and said, "Well, you see, my wife isn't being a biblical wife." Then he waited.

After a moment or so, I said, "Kyle, I'm not sure I know what you mean." I had an idea of what he was getting at, but I wanted him to tell me.

"Well, you know—she's not being biblical," he said with some frustration at me.

"No, I need you to be more specific," I answered.

"Well, she just won't be submissive to me," he finally blurted out.

His wife gave me a funny look and just rolled her eyes. It was clear that the more he had tried to get her to be submissive, the feistier she had become. I talked with her a bit about her own attitude, and then turned back and said to Kyle, "But how long has it been since you were submissive to your wife?"

He gave me a look that spoke more than words, and then asked, "Where do you get that idea? My Bible tells the wife to submit."

I agreed that the Bible does tell the wife to be submissive, but I pointed him to Ephesians 5:21 and asked him what he thought that meant. He had his Bible with him, so he looked it up to see if I was telling him the truth.

He read it over and over, and then finally said, "Huh, I never noticed that verse before. I'll have to think about that."

The principle Paul is giving us is that we are to be submissive to each other as unto the Lord. Then he goes into specific instructions for both husbands and wives. When this issue becomes a problem for a couple, perhaps instead of thinking about submission, we should think about humbling ourselves before the Lord.

Talking Together

What were some of the things you were taught about submission and marriage as you were growing up? Often we think we are the one doing the most submitting in our marriage. So instead, ask each other, "How much do you feel I demonstrate a submissive spirit in our marriage?"

Praying Together

Lord Jesus, You are the example of a submissive spirit.
You humbled Yourself and became like us so that You could die for
us. Your resurrection proved the power of Your submissive spirit,
and we thank You for that example. Help us have that same
spirit in our marriage, we pray.
Amen.

DAY 2

The Husband as the Head

You wives will submit to your husbands as you do to the Lord.
For a husband is the head of his wife as Christ is the head of his body,
the church; he gave his life to be her Savior.

EPHESIANS 5:22-23

When one thinks of headship in a corporate sense, being the head means you are the boss. This was the meaning Kyle attached to the idea of being the head of the house. However, while it is true that someone needs to be in charge, I don't believe this gives us the best understanding of what Paul is saying in these verses.

I remember reading about Lewis and Clark's exploration of the unexplored lands in the northwest part of our country. As they proceeded west, they came to the "headwaters" of the Missouri River. I've read also of those who have explored the "headwaters" of the mighty Amazon River in South America. The headwaters are the beginning of a river, or its "source." What if we were to think of "headship" of a family as similar to the "headwaters" of a river? If we took the concept of "headship" in a home in this light, we would be saying that the husband is the "source" of all that happens in the marriage and in the family.

Does that fit with what Paul is saying about Christ and His Body? We can say that Christ is the boss of the church, but when we look at the church and all the different directions in which it seems to be heading, it's hard to imagine there is a boss that is being followed. Yet if we think of Christ as the "source" of everything that the church, His Body, is meant to be, it makes sense. He is the "headwater" of the church—its beginning point.

Think of the implications of the husband being the "source," the one who sets the pace in the marriage. This certainly makes sense in what I've observed among couples. The wife may protest and say, "But I'm the one that takes care of everything. If I don't do it, nothing will happen. How can you say my husband is the 'source'?"

Well, who is setting the pace in that marriage? Obviously, in some cases, the husband is setting the pace by his inaction and passivity. If the husband is the "source," then whatever is going on in the marriage—good, frustrating, passive or bad—the husband is setting the pace for it.

Talking Together

In what ways do you see the husband setting the pace in your marriage? What are some of the good things your husband produces in your marriage through the role of being the "source"? In what ways does seeing Christ as the head, or the "source," help you better understand what a husband does?

Praying Together

Lord Jesus, You are the source of all that exists. We acknowledge You as the source for our marriage, for we want to be everything as a couple that we can possibly be. It's very easy to just go it alone and forget to trust You as our source, especially when we try to work things out between us. We need Your help to remember that You are everything that we need.
Amen.

DAY 3

The Husband Is a Sacrificial Lover

So Jacob spent the next seven years working to pay for Rachel. But his love for her was so strong that it seemed to him but a few days.

GENESIS 29:20

I love the stories of the patriarchs in Genesis. God allows us to see them in all of their humanness, and that not only helps us to understand them better but also helps us to understand ourselves better. Jacob was a conniver, and was his mother's favorite son. When he was growing up, Jacob probably lacked nothing and got everything he wanted, maybe even before he knew he wanted it. I'm sure Rebekah catered to his every need.

Yet, when Jacob met Rachel, and fell in love with her, he had to wait seven years for her to be his bride. He not only had to wait those seven years, he had to work for her father all those years. Every penny he earned stayed with his uncle, Laban, as payment for his bride-to-be. One of the most beautiful expressions of his love for Rachel is Jacob's statement that the seven years seemed as but a few days to him. What sacrificial love that was, and what an example to us husbands.

We, as husbands, are called to be sacrificial lovers. Paul tells us husbands that you "must love your wives with the same love Christ showed for the church" (Eph. 5:25). Then he goes on to point out that Christ died for the church. We get a better picture of how Christ loved the church in Philippians 2:5-11, a passage that many think was a hymn sung in the early church. In this passage, Paul urges us to have the same attitude as Christ, who gave up His rights as God, who became nothing, who took the humble position of slave, and who was humbly obedient even to the point of dying for us. That's an incredible example of what it means to be a husband!

The husband who loves his wife as Christ loved the church is willing to give up his right to be right; he is willing to humble himself; and he is also willing to not only die for his wife but also live for her. As I read these passages, it seems to me that the husband is called to a far greater degree of submissiveness than the wife, and if we have the attitude or mind of Christ in this, we find it a joy to love our wives in this way. Proverbs 15:33 reminds us husbands that "Humility precedes honor."

Talking Together

As the husband, take some time to talk to your wife about your response to Philippians 2:5-11. What is hard for you to accept? What is hard for you to act out in your daily life and marriage? How can your wife help you in this task?

Praying Together

*Father, You have given husbands a high calling. We are both
beginning to understand that the husband is to be the source for our
family. We, as husbands, are to be humble servants to our wives
and families. Yet, as in the example of Christ, when he had obeyed
and humbled himself to dying on the cross, You lifted him up
and gave him honor. As a husband and wife, we want You to lift
us up—we don't want to lift ourselves up. Help us as we humble
ourselves before each other and before You.
Amen.*

DAY 4

A Husband Is a Man of God

David found favor with God.
ACTS 7:46

When we think of a husband being a man of God, we may think of a man of God as being someone like Billy Graham, or Paul, or Peter, or one of the other disciples. However, the example in Scripture that stands out is King David. He was a "man after God's own heart." Yet he also was a great sinner. He committed adultery, which led to his committing murder. He had many women in his life—wives and concubines. His children had problems, and one turned against him and tried to take over the nation in the place of him. So how does David qualify as a "man of God"?

I often think of David in comparison with King Saul. Saul had none of the problems that David had. He had one wife and was apparently faithful to her. His son, Jonathan, was very loyal to him; his troops never rebelled against him; and his sin of disobedience seems so minor compared to David's bold sins. Yet God rejected Saul, and David "found favor with God." What was the difference between them?

I think the difference was in their response to confrontation. In 1 Samuel 15, Samuel confronts Saul for his disobedience, and when Saul rationalizes his behavior, Samuel tells him, "Obedience is far better than sacrifice" (1 Sam. 15:22). Then Saul admits that he disobeyed out of fear, asks for forgiveness, and then begs Samuel to make a sacrifice with him so that he looks good in front of his people. When confronted with his sin, Saul is more worried about appearance than about a soft heart that is open to repentance.

Look at what happens when the prophet Nathan confronts David. There is no rationalizing. There is only the quick recognition that not only did he sin against Bathsheba and her husband, Uriah, but even more importantly, as David says, "I have sinned against the Lord" (2 Sam. 12:13). It's as if Saul said, "Yes, but . . ." and David said, "Yes, I did!" The king that was rejected had a "manly heart" that was hardened against the recognition of his sin. David had a "godly heart" that understood the depth of his sin.

We learn more of David's heart in Psalm 51, when he writes, "For I recognize my shameful deeds—they haunt me day and night. Against you, and you alone, have I sinned" (vv. 3-4). A husband who is a man of God has a heart that is focused primarily on God, and his life will reflect that attitude in all that he is and does as a husband.

Talking Together

Read together 1 Samuel 15 and compare Saul's reaction to Samuel to what David writes in Psalm 51. What makes for a godly heart? Can you think of an example of times when your partner displayed a godly heart? How did it make you feel?

Praying Together

Lord, we both want godly hearts. We want You to be the primary focus of our lives, both individually and as a couple. Give us discerning eyes to see within ourselves the things that pull us away from You. Keep us from looking at our partner and judging his or her heart, and help us to understand better the role You set out for husbands in Scripture.

Amen.

DAY 5

A Husband Is a Sensitive Lover

I am my lover's, the one he desires.
SONG OF SONGS 7:10

Every couple should read Solomon's Song of Songs together at least once a month. While it is a sensuous love song between a husband and a wife, its metaphors are oriented to a different time and culture. Yet that can be part of the pleasure of reading it together—you can see if you can come up with more contemporary metaphors.

For centuries the only official interpretation of the Song of Songs was to think of this book as an allegory picturing Israel as God's espoused bride, or as a love song between Christ and the Church. Yet, the song depicts the actual wooing and real wedding of a shepherdess by her Shulamite lover, presumed to be Solomon. It progresses from wooing to the marriage, and then on to the struggles of love and the growing together that results from the struggles.

When I ask a couple, "What drew you, or attracted you, to each other at the beginning of your relationship?" their response often takes some time. Many times a couple will wrestle with this answer, for they have lost that sense of wonder and attraction—the struggles have limited their vision of the other person. Here is another place where the husband sets the tone. He needs to hold on to that sense of wonder at the beauty and uniqueness of his wife, as they grow old together. One of the most beautiful sights one can see is an older couple walking along hand in hand. The years may have changed their features, and even the shape of their bodies, but when they look at each other, they do so with a sense of awe.

I regularly try to look at Jan and wonder what life is like for her. I think things like, "I wonder what blue looks like to her? Is it different to her than to me? What goes through her mind when she looks at one of our grandchildren? Does love feel the same to her as to me, or is it different?" These are unanswerable questions that remind me of the mystery of our personhood. We are so complex as individuals that there is always something we can wonder about, and in that wondering stand in awe of the uniqueness of our partner.

The Shulamite and the shepherdess certainly had that sense of awe in their relationship. Yet then, of course, they were early in their marriage relationship. We need to guard against the charge leveled against the church in Ephesus, about whom Jesus said, "You don't love me or each other as you did at first! Look how far you have fallen from your first love! Turn back to me again" (Rev. 2:4-5). With a little effort, we can keep love alive over the years.

Talking Together

Talk together about what ways your love has grown. What still attracts you to your partner? What did you like about him or her in the early stages of your relationship?

Praying Together

Heavenly Father, we forget how complex we are as humans.
We really are fearfully and wonderfully made. Help us to never
lose that sense of awe at the complexity of our partner. Keep us
discovering new things about each other, and as we grow in our
love for each other, keep us growing in our love for You.
Amen.

DAY 6

A Husband Is Careful in His Behavior

Do not enter the path of the wicked, and do not walk in the way of evil.
Avoid it, do not travel on it; turn away from it and pass on.
PROVERBS 4:14-15, *NKJV*

Evil is seductive and never presents itself in any of its ugliness until we have been ensnared in its clutches. That's why we can never be too careful about our behavior.

Chris was weeping as he told me what had happened to him. He had been involved in a campus ministry along with his wife, Wanda. They had been working on several university campuses with students along with some other staff, and had been having a good ministry together.

During the past year, a female graduate student had started coming to his noon Bible study on campus. She wasn't a believer, but seemed very interested and wanted to learn more about the Bible. She had started to hang around after the study to ask Chris questions. She was a very attractive young woman, and Chris hadn't missed that fact. Yet this was evangelism, and he needed to be available.

He never noticed that he avoided telling Wanda about her. Even when he was late getting home several times, which had kept Wanda from something she had to do, he wasn't specific about whom he had been talking with.

When the young woman asked to meet with him at other times to discuss his faith, Chris thought he could handle things, not giving any credibility to his own feelings of attraction and how he looked forward to seeing this woman. Eventually they stopped talking about their faith, and started talking about each other. There were some hugs and a kiss, and then, overwhelmed by guilt, he confessed to his wife what he had been withholding from her. He told of his attraction to this woman and how sorry he was for betraying their marriage. Wanda was crushed.

Now, as he talked, he was completely confused—his feelings were in turmoil. He kept repeating, "How did this happen to me? I thought I could handle it." I pointed him to Proverbs, especially the fifth chapter. In that chapter we are told to run from evil—we aren't strong enough to withstand its temptations. There's good reason for us as men to be especially careful about our behaviors and to let our wives be "a fountain of blessing for [us]" (Prov. 5:18).

Talking Together

What have been some of the behavioral limits you have set for each other over the years? Who has been a positive influence for you both in setting standards of behavior for your marriage? In what ways has that been a blessing for you?

Praying Together

Lord, You have warned us that when we feel strong, we are to be careful, lest we fall. We don't want to resist Your guidance, though sometimes we do. Yet we don't want to be seduced by evil, either. Give us wisdom, eyes to see reality, and a loyal heart that keeps us careful in all of our behaviors.
Amen.

DAY 7

A Husband Is to Be Sympathetic

Why be so sad just because you have no children? You have me—
isn't that better than having ten sons?

1 SAMUEL 1:8

I know wives who would give anything to hear their husbands say something like what Elkanah said to Hannah. One translation says, "Isn't my love for you better than ten sons?" Elkanah had two wives, one named Peninnah, who had children, and the other named Hannah, who had no children. In that time, the way that you won your husband's heart was to have children. Yet not in Elkanah's case—his love was focused on Hannah.

Apparently Hannah didn't see Peninnah that often, but once each year they went up to Shiloh to worship and sacrifice to the Lord. All the way there, Peninnah would taunt Hannah about her barrenness. Hannah would be reduced to tears. Nothing Elkanah could say or do would help. He gave her the special portion of food, "because he loved her very much" (1 Sam. 1:5). Yet Hannah was so upset that she didn't even eat. Nothing could make up for her failure. In her mind, the only thing that mattered was to be able to have a son with Elkanah.

The account in 1 Samuel is important, for finally God gave Hannah a son, named Samuel. After he was weaned, she gave him literally to the Lord, and he became the greatest judge in Israel's history, and a pivotal person in the building of Israel as a nation.

How did Elkanah learn to be so sympathetic to his wife's painful situation? We really don't know that, or much else about him. Yet we do know that he loved his wife and paid close attention to what was going on with her emotionally.

I don't know that many men are ever good at being sympathetic. We can blame it on our culture, where men have been taught to be strong and unemotional in so many areas of their lives. However, I think men have always been that way to some degree. Men have to learn about sympathy and about emotions, and they usually do it within marriage. Many times, wives are the teachers. Even though men resist what their wives say, it still has its impact on them.

I also think that we, as husbands, can benefit from the example of older, wiser, more mellow men in our lives. Sometimes our fathers can fill this role, but usually it is someone else that we respect. We need to be open to these mentors and listen to them so that we can learn more about sympathy. It is a manly trait.

Talking Together

Talk together about your husband's ability to express sympathy to you, his wife. In what situations has he been most sympathetic? How have you been able to help each other understand more about sympathy?

Praying Together

Lord Jesus, as we look at Your life on earth, we can learn from You as we see that You showed great sympathy. Help us also to be open to learning and growing in this area through our human relationships. Help us to limit our time with those who are callous and unsympathetic, and put people in our lives who will help us grow in the direction You want to see us go.
Amen.

THE WIFE'S ROLE

DAY 1

A Wife Is Gentle, but Strong

She is clothed with strength and dignity, and she laughs with no fear of the future. When she speaks, her words are wise, and kindness is the rule when she gives instructions.
PROVERBS 31:25-26

We often set up the Proverbs 31 woman to be the ideal wife. In some ways she is, but I often wonder when she sleeps. I often wonder how many men could accept a woman that competent. She seems to be a workaholic, both at home and in business. Yet that doesn't take away from the nobility of her character as it serves as a model for wives today. One of the concepts she illustrates is the balance between tender and tough.

Earl was married to a Proverbs 31 wife. She was superwoman, and he had a hard time keeping up with her. He was ready for retirement and she was in the throes of getting her business launched. Kristine was animated when she talked about her new business, but lost interest when she talked about Earl or about the kids.

"See," Earl noted, "that's what bugs me. I'm ready to slow down and start having some fun, and her fun is all wrapped up in her business. That's all she thinks about, day and night. I really don't know where I fit in anymore."

"Well, I need you in the business," Kristine replied. "I can use you there to help me and it would be fun to work together."

However, Earl wasn't buying it. "She's only partly a Proverbs 31 woman," he finally said. "She knows how to be the businesswoman, but she's forgotten how to be the wife."

It was obvious where Kristine's heart was. She was totally consumed by her new business. She got lots of strokes from her clients, for she did a great job. "She's always been competent at everything she's done," Earl said. "But now she's forgotten how to be a wife and mother. I don't see her gentle spirit anymore, and I really miss that part of her."

Can a woman be too strong? It isn't easy for any woman to balance tenderness with toughness. The tender heart in a woman imitates closely the tender heart of God. Yet God models toughness, too, and women need to do the tough work of setting limits when they are called for. The Godly woman never loses sight of the need to balance her gentleness with her strength.

Talking Together

Some couples balance tender and tough by the husband being tough and the wife being tender. That doesn't really work. Tenderness and toughness are important for both husband and wife. How have you been able to balance these opposite, but necessary, qualities in your marriage? How can you help each other better maintain a balance?

Praying Together

Father, we want to be able to balance tenderness and toughness within each of us. You model for us throughout Scripture Your tender, gentle heart, and yet You show toughness as You set limits on our behaviors. You do both of these things because You love us. Give us patience with each other. Help each of us to affirm our strengths, and encourage us in the areas that need growth. We thank You for caring about these things.
Amen.

DAY 2

A Wife Is a Helpmate

Who can find a virtuous and capable wife? She is worth more than
precious rubies. Her husband can trust her, and she will greatly enrich his life.
She will not hinder him but help him all her life.

PROVERBS 31:10-12

This passage in Proverbs 31 echoes the words of Genesis 2, where God says that "It is not good for the man to be alone. I will make a companion who will help him" (Gen. 2:18). Thus, Eve was created to be a helpmate for Adam. The old saying that "behind every successful man is a good woman" is still true. That's the whole point of a wife being a helpmate.

Fritz was the CEO of his company, and they were working on taking the company public. His hours at work expanded due to meetings with the people who were helping them in that process. Peggy took care of the house and the kids and enjoyed being at home. "I understand what he's going through and I support him," she told me. "I know his priorities are at home with us, but right now the demands of the business are heavy and he has to put in long hours. Maybe after they go public, he'll be able to cut back some and spend more time with us."

"I really appreciate her support," Fritz added. "Over the years of our marriage we've both had situations when extra demands were placed on one of us and the other chipped in more to keep things going. I've never had any doubts about Peggy's support."

I thought about what they both had said and felt that Fritz could identify with Proverbs 12:4: "A worthy wife is her husband's joy and crown." They had developed a real sense of teamwork as a couple.

Peggy had had a great career of her own. She had been a CPA when they married and had a good business of her own going. Yet, when she became pregnant with their first child, she made the decision, with Fritz's support, to stay at home. The mutual respect they had for each other kept them working as a team, regardless of what was going on in their careers.

A wife can make or break her husband by her support or lack of support. That's not to blame her for his problems—it's just to make clear that her role, whether at home or at the office, is a critical part of her husband's success. That's the way God designed it.

Talking Together

Discuss what you think it means to be a "helpmate." In what ways have you been helpers to each other? How can you stay sensitive to each other's needs in the future?

Praying Together

*Lord Jesus, help us to be more sensitive to each other's needs
and to learn how to be real helpers to each other. Help us both to be
sensitive to times when the balance shifts and more help is needed
from one of us for a time. May we learn to follow the plan You
set out for a husband and a wife to be mutually responsible
for the work in our marriage.*
Amen.

DAY 3

A Wife Respects Her Husband

Each man must love his wife as he loves himself,
and the wife must respect her husband.
EPHESIANS 5:33

When a wife is cherished and feels loved by her husband, she flourishes. In the same way, when a husband feels that his wife respects him, he, too, flourishes. When he senses his wife has lost respect for him, he crumbles—even when he has done something to cause her to lose respect for him. A wife, also, when she is not made to feel special and given first place in her husband's priorities, crumbles. That seems to be God's order of things. A wife needs to be cherished and loved; a husband needs to be respected.

Carrie was very up front about the fact that she didn't respect Sam anymore. "He lies to me, and he never follows through on anything. He stays at work just to avoid me," she said very clearly. She meant it, and Sam knew that she felt that way. He sat there like a whipped puppy—he didn't seem to care anymore about what Carrie said or felt.

"Yeah, I know she feels that way. She makes it clear to me just about every day that she has no respect for me." Then, after a moment, Sam added, "I just don't know where to begin. I don't know what I can do that will make any difference." Then he closed up again. It was also clear that Sam no longer communicated to Carrie that she was number-one in his priority list.

Carrie said, "I know I'm like the wife in Proverbs who nags so much she's like the constant dripping of rain [see Prov. 27:15], but I don't know what to do, either. I just don't know how to change things for the better."

Sam and Carrie were in a tough spot, for unless they could find some way for him to regain her respect, things would just keep getting worse. Finally, I suggested that Carrie make a list of all the things that Sam still did that were moral, ethical and helpful. I asked her if she could do that. She thought awhile and then agreed. Later, when she showed us her list, Sam started to perk up. There were things that Carrie had to admit Sam did well. He was a good father. He was sincere in his desire to please the Lord. And what she considered lies were often misunderstandings. Gradually, Carrie started to take her focus off of all the things that Sam did wrong, or didn't do at all, and instead focus on what Sam did that was right and helpful. And Sam began to work on making Carrie his first priority. Together, they were able to start a new, constructive cycle. A wife's respect for her husband is a powerful motivator.

Talking Together

How true is it that you as a wife respond to cherishing and being loved by your husband, and that you as a husband respond to being respected by your wife? Give an example of a time you experienced this in your marriage. Can you think of other ways you could let each other know that you need either more respect or more cherishing?

Praying Together

Father, we know what we need to do for each other, but sometimes it is difficult to do it. We need Your help here. Help me as a husband to love and cherish my wife more, and help me as a wife to respect my husband more. Give us both the ability to be able to recognize these things when they are given.
Amen.

DAY 4

A Wife Is a Woman of God

*Charm is deceptive, and beauty does not last; but a woman
who fears the Lord will be greatly praised.*

PROVERBS 31:30

We are all created in the image of God. That means that the person
sleeping next to you reflects back to you some aspect of God's character. None of us are perfect reflectors, but we all reflect some aspect
of God. Perhaps that is why we are so often drawn to our opposite in
choosing a marriage partner—we each reflect a different part of God
to the other.

One of the things that wives are called to reflect to their husbands is a picture of God's mercy. A wife does this through her tenderness and compassion. Peter reminds wives of this in his first letter.
He speaks to the woman who is married to an unbeliever and suggests, "your godly lives will speak to them better than any words. They
will be won over by watching your pure, godly behavior" (1 Pet. 3:1-2).

I reminded Janet of this. She had been talking to me about her
unbelieving husband. "He knows the truth about salvation. He's just
too bullheaded to let anyone else tell him about something that's
good for him."

I asked her if she was continuing to pressure him. She answered,
"Only at certain times. He goes to church with me, and if the sermon
applies to him, I'll tell him so. He just clams up when I do that."

I pointed her to 1 Peter 3 and asked if she had considered that as
a strategy to use with her husband. "I've thought about it, but I just
don't have the patience to do that," she answered. When I asked her
how long he'd been resisting her efforts, she said, "Oh, we've been
married thirty years and I became a Christian the first year of mar-

riage. So I guess it's been twenty-nine years."

"You've been too patient," I told her. "It's time you tried a new strategy—one that God endorses. Why not try to win him with your godly behavior?"

There was silence for a while, and then she said, "I guess I'm afraid I'm not godly enough." I told her she might be surprised, especially if she focused more on how the unstated messages she gave impacted him. That's good advice even for wives married to believers.

Talking Together

Talk together about what each of you thinks is godly behavior. In what ways might you demonstrate godly behavior to your mate? How do these behaviors strengthen your marriage?

Praying Together

Heavenly Father, we want to be more godly in our behavior.
This isn't something that is emphasized much in our culture,
but we desire it as a couple. Show us areas we need to change
as well as areas in which we need to grow. Help us to become
what You want us to be together.
Amen.

DAY 5

A Wife Knows Her Unfading Beauty Is Within

*Don't be concerned about the outward beauty that depends on
fancy hairstyles, expensive jewelry, or beautiful clothes. You should be
known for the beauty that comes from within, the unfading beauty of a
gentle and quiet spirit, which is so precious to God.*

1 PETER 3:3-4

This is an interesting passage. One can read it and get very upset by anyone who uses external things to enhance his or her appearance. Some Christians have taken these words very literally and forbidden the wearing of jewelry and emphasized plain clothing. Other Christians have ignored these words and done everything they could humanly do to improve their appearance, including plastic surgery. The sad thing is that both of these behaviors are errors that miss the central teaching of this passage.

Peter is not as concerned with the externals as he is with the internals. His point is that wives should be recognized for an internal beauty. That's far more important than what they do or don't do to enhance their external appearances.

I've listened to wives tear themselves down in front of their husbands. They point out the changes that have taken place over the years—the extra weight that won't go away, the wrinkles in the face, and even the tiredness that comes with raising children or teenagers. I've even seen husbands cry as they try to reassure their wives that they are not turned off by the externals of their wives' appearances. They even argue with their wives about how good they look and yet their wives insist that they are lying.

Somewhere along the way, these wives have lost sight of the importance of internal beauty that Peter seems to think is so important, even though their husbands not only see the internal beauty, but also still see their wives as beautiful on the outside.

Maybe the wife like this was raised in a home where she was made fun of by her brothers or her father or mother. Maybe her husband has been too silent over the years and forgotten to affirm his continued attraction to his wife because of who she is. Maybe she can't see anything good in herself for a variety of other reasons. Yet, whatever the reason, she needs to focus on building up her inner beauty. She needs to see herself as God sees her—a precious child of His, for whom Christ died on the cross.

God loves us just as we are, and that love stirs up the reality of the inner beauty, which is reflected in the external beauty as well.

Talking Together

Talk together about how you, as the wife, view your physical body. Together describe some of the marks of her inner beauty.

Praying Together

Father, we know You don't make junk, but sometimes we feel like we are just junk. Forgive us for those thoughts and help us to see ourselves as You see us—through the eyes of love. Help us to be aware of those facets of inner beauty we reflect, and may that awareness grow within us as we become more like You.

Amen.

DAY 6

A Wife Is Submissive

As the church submits to Christ, so you wives must submit to
your husbands in everything.

EPHESIANS 5:24

Remember, the principle is in verse 21 of Ephesians 5—both husbands and wives are to submit to each other out of reverence for Christ. Yet Paul, like Peter, makes it a point to remind wives to submit to their husbands. I've often wondered if the early church was struggling with the new equality given to women. Maybe Paul was encouraging wives not to forget that submission was still important.

There is a wonderful old essay written by a secular family therapist entitled "The Power Tactics of Jesus." In this essay, Jay Haley looks at Jesus' behavior, in particular His behavior after He was arrested by the Jewish leaders. All through the three different trials to which Jesus is subjected, He is submissive to the authorities, but He is also very much in control of Himself. In His trial before Pilate, Jesus' submissiveness is especially clearly shown. It is seen in His response to Pilate's questions.

Pilate asks, "Are you the King of the Jews?"

Jesus answers back passively, "Yes, it is as you say."

Then Pilate asks, " 'Aren't you going to say something? What about all these charges against you?' But Jesus said nothing, much to Pilate's surprise" (Mark 15:2-5).

In John's account, he adds an important exchange between Jesus and Pilate. Pilate asks Jesus,

> "Where are you from?" But Jesus gave no answer. "You won't talk to me?" Pilate demanded. "Don't you realize that I have the power to release you or to crucify you?"

Then Jesus said, "you would have no power over me at all unless it were given to you from above. So the one who brought me to you has the greater sin" (John 19:9-11).

Who is in control in this situation? Obviously Jesus. Haley notes that Jesus is the one with the real power in this situation. His power is expressed in His submissiveness. In the same way, we can experience a sense of power in our submissive spirit within our marriage, and we need to be careful that our submission is really "as unto Christ." When we humble ourselves before the Lord, we need to recognize how submission can be used as a power move, and give up that power. When we do that, we will understand the true nature of the submissive spirit.

Talking Together

In what ways do you think submission might be used as a power tactic? How can a wife be submissive without it being a power move? Talk with each other about submissiveness and how it can enhance your marriage.

Praying Together

Lord Jesus, we want to be submissive to You and Your will. We don't want to use submission as a power play, but we are human and do that at times. Help us to submit to each other, not as a power move, but as we submit to You.

Amen.

DAY 7

A Wife Is a Woman of Influence

In the same way, their wives must be respected and must not speak evil of others.
They must exercise self-control and be faithful in everything they do.
1 TIMOTHY 3:11

In this passage, Paul is giving instructions to the leaders in the early church. He goes into detail regarding the standards for the husbands, and then adds these words regarding the leaders' wives. Obviously, how they behaved had a bearing on their husbands' qualifications for leadership.

An interesting piece of information regarding a wife's influence in her marriage has been noted recently. It appears that in marriages that succeed, one of the key factors in that success is the ability of the wife to influence her husband on matters. One major newspaper reported on this research under a headline saying, "Marriages succeed when the husband does what his wife tells him to do." They totally missed the point. It's not that the husband does what his wife says all the time, but that he listens to her and accepts and is influenced by what she says.

So now research verifies what many wives have said all along. The wise husband will take seriously what his wife tells him. He needn't always do what she says; yet he should be influenced by what she says.

This means, on the other hand, that marriages often fail when the husband doesn't give validity to what his wife says. The husband who believes that he alone knows what is best is heading for marital problems, and even marital breakup. So is the husband who thinks that headship makes him the boss.

What was also interesting in this study was that it showed that it didn't make any difference in terms of the success of the marriage if the wife was influenced by the husband. Only when the husband was influenced by the wife did it matter. Jan and I are not sure how that plays out, but I really try to take what my wife says seriously. There have been many times when I haven't really acted on what she has said, and then found out later that she was right. Remember, a wife's influence is not only an important part of her contribution to the marriage; it also makes for a successful marriage relationship.

Talking Together

A husband may think he takes his wife's contributions seriously, but it matters more whether a wife thinks she is being taken seriously. How has this worked in your marriage? Who influences whom the most? What would it look like in your marriage if there was more of a balance regarding influence?

Praying Together

Heavenly Father, we want to be open to each other, and we now understand how important it is for the husband to be open to his wife's influence. Help us in this area of communication to be what You want us to be—sensitive and responsive to each other. Help us each to value what the other says and to remember that You will honor us as we honor each other's opinions.

Amen.

BUILDING TRUST

DAY 1

Trust Is Built on Honesty

Truth springs up from the earth, and righteousness smiles down from heaven.
Yes, the Lord pours down his blessings.
PSALM 85:11-12

What the psalmist is saying is that when truth is spoken here on earth, God smiles down on us from heaven. To make the point even more clear, he adds that the Lord also pours down His blessings. Yet truth is an elusive target in our marriages. Couples will lie to each other for good reasons. Some lie because they know how sensitive their partner is and they don't want to cause hurt. Other lies may be more playful, such as when we exaggerate a compliment to make our partner feel good. Even couples that claim to be very honest in their marriage will sometimes lie to those they love.

Terry is an example of a husband who lied out of love. He noted that throughout most of their marriage, he had lied by withholding the truth from Samantha. "I don't like conflict," he added. "So when it looked like we were heading for a conflict, I would just back down and say everything was okay." He had avoided the conflict, but had paid a heavy price for it.

Samantha responded to Terry's confession. "I knew it wasn't always okay, but I didn't know how to get him to open up. Over time I just learned not to believe him in those situations, and eventually to just disregard most of everything he would say. I don't trust him anymore."

How sad. Here was a behavior that was based on love, but not on truth, and it eventually led to distrust. Now Samantha and Terry were questioning just about everything in their relationship.

Building a truthful relationship takes work on the part of both the speaker and the listener. Often the listener gives the message that he or she doesn't really know how to handle the truth. If we are going to commit ourselves to being more honest with each other, we also must commit ourselves to working hard at eliminating our defensive posture when our partner is telling us the truth. Perhaps that's the harder assignment, but a relationship of trust built on truth takes work on both sides. Try in some small way to build this into your conversation together this week.

Talking Together

Think of some innocent ways you have hedged on the truth with each other. Why do you think you do that? Have you ever backed yourself into a corner by not telling the clear truth? What is the hardest part about hearing the truth?

Praying Together

Lord, You have promised that when truth springs up between us,
You smile in approval. Furthermore, You not only smile on us,
You pour out blessings on us. Give us the courage to be more
truthful, even about the little things. Help us to speak the truth
in love so that we can help each other be better listeners.
Amen.

DAY 2

Trust Is Maintained by Predictability

He will shield you with his wings. He will shelter you with his feathers.
His faithful promises are your armor and protection.
PSALM 91:4

Some people are born to be unpredictable. Routine, for them, is a sign of death, or at least of despair. To try and lock them into a predictable pattern would be like trying to cage a wild animal—they will kick against the restrictions even if they agree with them. They just don't like having their options taken away.

How does one learn to trust a person like that, especially if trust is maintained by predictability? For one thing, there is often a predictable pattern in these persons' unpredictability. If you're married to someone like this, you can learn what to expect, and there is some comfort in that.

Neal had this kind of personality. He might say he was going to the grocery store and then, two hours later, come home with a new TV. "Well," he would say, "I started out heading to the grocery store, and then remembered the appliance store was having a big sale and we had talked about a new TV." Predictable? To his wife it was. "He does that often—starts out to do one thing and ends up doing something else. I've learned to just roll with it, for I trust his heart, and his heart is very stable and predictable." As Neal listened, he smiled and reached over for her hand.

Predictability isn't limited to just behaviors. Someone's behaviors may fit into a highly predictable pattern, yet his or her heart may be somewhere else. Others, like Neal, are spontaneous in their behaviors, but steady as a rock in their hearts. Trust is a matter of the heart.

The psalmist says that "faithful promises are your armor and protection." That's a heart matter. If I know where your heart is—in being faithful to your promises—I can trust you. Yet if I sense you are wavering in your promises, then, regardless of your behavior, I will begin to question your trustworthiness. Remember, Jesus said our heart will always be where our treasure is, and if we treasure our partner, that's where our heart will be—predictable, year after year after year.

Talking Together

In what ways are you each predictable to the other? Do you enjoy routine, or do you feel like routine is boring and restricting? How do you gauge where your partner's heart is at any given point in time? Talk about the issue of predictability in your marriage.

Praying Together

Lord, You are always predictable, for Your promises to us are always certain. We acknowledge that Your promises are our armor and protection. We also want that same dependable feeling in our marriage relationship. Help us grow in this area.
Help us to treasure each other.
Amen.

DAY 3

Trust Comes Through Facing the Pain

You can't heal a wound by saying it's not there!
JEREMIAH 6:14, *TLB*

Someone once asked me why counseling dealt with only painful is-sues. Judy might have asked that question. She and her husband came to see me regarding some of their marital issues. It soon became very clear that she struggled with some very painful situations in her past. As we started to talk about these, she became very uncomfortable and could hardly sit still in her chair. "Why do we have to talk about these things?" she asked. "They're all in the past—I just want to forget they ever happened."

I could understand her discomfort, and told her so. Yet I then went on to point out how these issues were operating in her present situation, and in particular how they were affecting the way she was relating to her husband.

Based on the events about which we were talking, she had formed a very poor image of herself. She was also turning fifty soon and felt she was old and fat. She said she felt unworthy of her husband and even of her children. "Why is this hitting me now?" she finally asked.

One thing I've noticed over the years of working with people is that the way some cope with painful issues is effective only for a time. If we use denial, as Judy did, we can shut out those things from our awareness, and even shut them out of our relationships. Yet about the time we hit midlife, the coping skills that have been quite effective to this point begin to break down. They no longer work. Gradually what we have been avoiding for years now begins to surface in our rela-tionships, and seems to bubble up inside of us and hit us squarely in the face.

I said to her, "Looks like it's time for you to get through these painful issues. God has a way of bringing them before us, but He also has a way of healing those painful parts of us as we put them on the table and start to face the pain." I said all this in front of her husband, for I wanted him to know the pain she was feeling as well. How important it is to have our spouse walk alongside of us in the process of dealing with the past.

Talking Together

How do you each deal with physical pain? Do you deal with emotional pain the same way? How could you help each other better deal with the painful things you have experienced?

Praying Together

Lord Jesus, You know what pain is. You suffered on our behalf not only the physical pain of the cross but also the emotional pain of the Father's abandonment. We thank You for that. Help us to face any painful wounds in our past so that we can experience Your healing and deliverance. Help us also to stand by each other as we go through the healing process.

Amen.

DAY 4

Trust Is Synonymous with Love

Unfailing love and truth have met together. Righteousness and peace have kissed!
PSALM 85:10

In our workshops I often give a brief overview of the early stages of human development. I show that in the first months of an infant's life, the primary parental task is to make this new world seem safe to the infant. This is done through the emotion of love, which is movement toward someone. If the parents show love, the developing child learns how to trust others. Mom is the primary parent for this task, since she was the one that was there even before the birth.

Out of that we see that the first task for the infant is to experience unconditional love so that he or she can form a trusting relationship with someone who will make this world feel safer. Learning to trust is the most foundational truth that a child needs to experience, and it is experienced through being loved. If this experience of being loved is flawed, then it will create ongoing problems with trust in our adult relationships. Love teaches us to trust, so we could even say that love and trust are synonymous. In fact, one can take the passage in 1 John 4:20 and substitute the word "trust" where the word "love" is used, and have it reveal the same important truth.

Here's how it goes: "If someone says, 'I trust God,' but doesn't trust his Christian brother or sister, that person is a liar; for if we don't trust people we can see, how can we trust God, whom we have not seen?" It's easy to say we trust God when things are going well, but what happens when life starts to fall apart? Where does trust go then? All too often our ability to trust God disappears.

If we look further, we will usually see that someone who no longer trusts God when things are tough really doesn't know how to trust people. He or she also doesn't know how to trust anyone on a human level. What's the solution for such a person? Lots and lots of love. Lots and lots of grace. This grace must be extended when trust is broken so that we can learn how to repair trust and to receive the love and grace that is being given to us.

Talking Together

Talk together about what some of your trust issues are. Who do you trust? What makes it difficult for you to trust other people? How do you think your early experiences shaped your ability to trust?

Praying Together

Father, we want to be able to trust You more. We know that
You are trustworthy, but we sometimes still struggle with our
ability to trust even You. Help us to have the courage to look at how
we may have been affected by the way we learned to trust and to re-
ceive love as children. Give us a deeper understanding of
how much You love us, and help us also to know better
how to love each other.
Amen.

DAY 5

Trust Is Easily Broken

Have mercy on me, O God, because of your unfailing love.
Because of your great compassion, blot out the stain of my sins.
Wash me clean from my guilt. Purify me from my sin.
PSALM 51:1-2

I am certain that when King David looked down from his roof and began to lust after another man's wife, he never thought of the consequences. He expected that it would be a one-night fling; he never thought that the woman would get pregnant. Neither did he think, when he set up her husband to be killed, that there would be any consequences—after all, he was the king.

In all my years of working with couples, I have yet to talk with a husband or a wife who has been unfaithful to his or her partner who has said that he or she sat down beforehand and said to him or herself, "I know this is going to create all kinds of problems in my marriage and within me, but I'm going to do it anyway." Instead, they say that they were usually suffering from a severe form of crazy thinking, with all reason and all rationality having flown out of their minds. Perhaps that's part of the reason that Proverbs 5 and 7 advise the man who is tempted to run!

Trust is suddenly broken in this kind of situation. It isn't that trust gradually erodes—it is destroyed instantly. Harold talked to me about what he felt, months after finding out that his wife was involved in an affair. We had spent those months working together to restore their marriage, and it had gone well. They had even had their pastor perform a small ceremony where they renewed their vows. Yet this time, Harold was talking to me alone.

"I'm still having difficulty trusting her," he said. "How do I know that sometime in the future she will not do the same thing to me?" His questions were sincere, and I had no argument with what he was feeling. I could not offer him any assurance that what he feared would not happen again. I did say, though, that he needed more time. I reminded him that what is broken in an instant cannot be repaired in an instant, and that it might take several years for him to regain the ability to trust her. However, I added, "Don't rush the process—just stay with it and watch God at work!"

Talking Together

What behaviors or attitudes help you keep your trust of your partner strong? Talk about how someone could rebuild trust after it has been broken.

Praying Together

Lord God, we acknowledge that You are always faithful and therefore always trustworthy. Yet sometimes our expectations get in the way and we are disappointed because we don't see You act or intervene as we think You should. Forgive us for that and help us to rest in Your trustworthiness. Help us to keep our promises to each other.
Amen.

DAY 6

It Is Time-Consuming to Rebuild Trust

Purify me from my sins, and I will be clean; wash me, and I will be whiter
than snow. Oh, give me back my joy again; you have broken me.
PSALM 51:7-8

It is so true—it takes time to rebuild trust. What is broken in a split-second may take several years to restore. Yet it can be rebuilt, and it is usually rebuilt on our brokenness. The dash after David's words, "you have broken me" would indicate to me that he was too broken at that point to go on. Only after he had regained his composure could he write the next line: Now let me rejoice.

Russ and Erin's problems were great. Both were experiencing intense pain. Russ had lied to Erin about his work situation. He had said he had been promoted, when actually he had been demoted. It took Erin several months to find out the truth, and that was long after she had told everyone about his promotion. Now she felt foolish, and her trust in Russ was seriously damaged.

Russ was frustrated by it all. He didn't really understand what Erin was feeling. "It isn't that big a deal. I would have been promoted, but business is down and they made cutbacks, and at least I wasn't laid off like some others were. I just don't get it," he added. Through her tears, Erin affirmed, "Yes, that's right! You just don't get it!"

I pointed out to Russ that Erin's trust in him had been broken. "Doesn't that bother you?" I asked. His response wasn't designed to rebuild trust: "No, it doesn't. That's her problem and she just needs to get over it!" With that he withdrew into the corner of the couch.

Regardless of what any of us has done to break trust, we need to approach our partner with humility that leads to godly sorrow, and a willingness to do whatever it takes to restore the trust. King David said later, "Restore to me again the joy of your salvation, and make me willing to obey you" (v. 12). He knew it would take time, and he came before the Lord with genuine sorrow. He's our model for restoring broken trust—whatever the cause.

Talking Together

Talk about how important it is to know how deeply your partner trusts you. Even "little" things can injure trust. Talk about the daily things your partner does to keep trust strong.

Praying Together

Father, we come to You with hearts that never want to feel the pain that King David was feeling. We want to guard our trust with each other and we want to be faithful to our vows. Give us a sensitivity to each other that keeps us accountable. Thank You for Your faithfulness and trustworthiness.
Amen.

DAY 7

Trust Is the Foundation for a Healthy Marriage

Whatever we do, it is because Christ's love controls us. Since we believe that Christ died for everyone, we also believe that we have all died to the old life we used to live.

2 CORINTHIANS 5:14

There are a number of building blocks in the foundation of a healthy, growing marriage. One of the key blocks is the issue of trust. Mutual trust is necessary in order for a couple to be able to relax and enjoy one another.

One of the interesting marriages in the Old Testament is that of Boaz to Ruth. As I read through the account, I am impressed by the trusting relationship between Ruth and her mother-in-law, Naomi. Yet I am also impressed by the trust that developed between Ruth and Boaz. Boaz was a relative of Naomi's husband and was a kind man.

When Ruth began to gather the leftover grain in Boaz's field, Boaz inquired about her. He already knew of her loyalty to his sister-in-law Naomi. He allowed her to pick up the leftover grain, he fed her, and then he told his workers to let some extra grain fall on the ground on purpose for Ruth to pick up. Eventually, when Naomi thought it was time for Ruth to find a home, she told Ruth exactly what to do with Boaz, and again Ruth trusted her completely.

Ruth was a Moabite—a pagan woman who left her old life behind and came to the land of Judah with her mother-in-law after Ruth's husband died. She "died to her old life" and ventured out into the unknown, trusting her mother-in-law. She did what Naomi told her to do, which was to take a bath, get dressed up, and put on some great perfume. Then, she was told that after Boaz went to sleep, she was to go and lay down at his feet. She had to trust Naomi and Boaz, to be willing to do all of that.

Boaz was very kind to her, guarding her honor and giving her extra food to take back to Naomi. That same day, the marriage of Ruth and Boaz was worked out. Soon after the marriage, Ruth got pregnant and they had a son named Obed, who became the grandfather of King David.

We don't know much about their marriage, apart from the birth of their son. Yet the trustworthiness of both Boaz and Ruth was a strong predictor of a healthy marriage. Mutual trustworthiness in any marriage will lay the foundation not only for health, but also for joy.

Talking Together

Read together the book of Ruth and look for ways each of the three main characters displayed trustworthiness. In what ways do you each demonstrate trustworthiness to your partner? Talk about any areas that need to be strengthened.

Praying Together

*Heavenly Father, we know there are always ways we can
become more trustworthy. Because of our humanness, we need
help in this area. Give us patience with each other. Help us to see
this area of our marriage through the eyes of grace. May we feel
Your loving hand upholding us as a couple.
Amen.*

OFFERING FORGIVENESS

DAY 1

Forgiveness Is to Be Our Lifestyle

You must make allowance for each other's faults and forgive the person who offends you. Remember, the Lord forgave you, so you must forgive others.

COLOSSIANS 3:13

Forgiveness goes against the grain of our human emotions. We would much rather think in terms of revenge. When we have been wronged, there is a false sense of power in thinking of getting even, or even just in holding on to the grudge. Yet that should not be our choice. Paul is very clear in several places that we must make allowances and we must forgive.

I've never heard this Colossians passage used as a text for a wedding sermon, but it certainly applies to marriage. One can even think of marriage as a school for forgiveness. Put two people into a close, committed relationship and conflict will occur, and where there is conflict, there must also be forgiveness.

A basic biblical definition of forgiveness is to "cancel a debt." When we forgive our partner, we are releasing him or her from owing us anything. We are both then able to walk around debt-free, at least in terms of our marriage relationship.

How different Jesus' teaching on forgiveness was from the Jewish teaching of that day (and also of today). When Peter asked Jesus how many times he should forgive someone, Peter very graciously offered a suggestion that it might be "seven times" (Matt. 18:21). His offer was gracious because he had been taught by the rabbis that you had to forgive someone only three times, and then only if they repented. After that, you no longer needed to forgive that person. As Peter saw it, one was supposed to forgive, but only up to a point.

Peter was in no way prepared for Jesus' answer: "No, Peter, not seven times, but seventy times seven" (see Matt. 18:22). That's 490 times. That should cover any marriage relationship!

When we forgive someone, we are giving ourselves a gift, for when we forgive, we find freedom.

Talking Together

What have been your thoughts about the extent of our forgiving? Who in your life do you find it difficult to forgive? How forgiving have you been in your marriage? Talk about whether forgiveness is withheld or not when the offender has not repented.

Praying Together

Father in heaven, we are so grateful that You have forgiven us. You forgive freely and completely. Sometimes we don't follow Your example and are stingy with our forgiveness because we don't understand fully Your forgiveness of us or that it frees us to cancel a debt. Help us to live a lifestyle of forgiveness and in that way to honor You for forgiving us.
Amen.

DAY 2

Our Forgiveness Is to Be Unlimited

And forgive us our sins, just as we have forgiven those who have sinned against us.
MATTHEW 6:12

I say that our forgiving is to be unlimited simply because we want God to be unlimited in His forgiveness of us. Jesus, in teaching us the Lord's Prayer, gives us the means to experience God's unlimited forgiveness. It is based on our forgiveness of others.

Carey and Yolanda were in the recovery stage of dealing with Carey's affair. He had made good progress in showing genuine sorrow over what he had done and in being accountable to his wife, and he really was trying to be more the husband Yolanda had always wanted him to be. On her part, Yolanda had pretty well worked through her forgiveness of his act.

In one of our meetings, Yolanda took both of us by surprise—we had no idea what she was about to say. As we were talking, she said, "I have something important to say and it is very difficult for me to say it, but I feel I need to." She then went on to confess to Carey that twelve years earlier she had had a brief affair with a young man. Both Carey and I sat there in complete shock.

Carey's first response was simply to say, "Wow, I need to think this through." I don't remember what else we talked about, but at our next meeting, Carey announced that he needed to separate from Yolanda. He had been totally shocked at her revelation and didn't think he could ever get over her violation of trust. Even though I reminded him of the reason we were meeting together—his own affair—he was adamant that they separate and take a break from our meetings. Yolanda sat there in disbelief. Then she got angry and stormed out of the room in tears.

Carey just sat there, so I asked him what was so different about what she had done years ago and what he had done months ago. He couldn't give me an answer. He just said, "Somehow, it's different to me." I was tempted to point out the old double standard, but decided instead to talk to him about forgiveness. He didn't change his mind, even though I clearly reiterated to him what Jesus had said after He gave the disciples that prayer. He didn't understand that there is nothing that ever happens in families that is beyond forgiveness. That's a true statement because of how much God has forgiven us!

Talking Together

Talk together about times when it has been hard for you to forgive someone. What made it possible for you to finally forgive that person? What are some of the hurdles you still feel you encounter when it comes to forgiving?

Praying Together

Father, it is a heavy responsibility to always forgive. Yet we know that You forgave us when we didn't deserve it and when we were even rebellious against You. Help us keep short accounts in our forgiving. Keep us ever mindful of what it cost You to forgive us. Amen.

DAY 3

Forgiveness Isn't an Option

If you forgive those who sin against you, your heavenly Father will forgive you.
But if you refuse to forgive others, your Father will not forgive your sins.
MATTHEW 6:14-15

Jesus' words here are very clear and direct. He doesn't leave anything in question. We either forgive everything that happens in our lives, or we are not going to be forgiven ourselves. I've often asked audience members to describe what is unforgivable for us as humans. The answers are usually the same: murder, especially of a child; sexual abuse; an affair; rape; and the physical abuse of a child or of an elderly person.

Are these really unforgivable? Not according to what Jesus is saying. There don't seem to be any exceptions to His statement. Some years ago, a young man shot and killed his wife and then tried to kill himself. He failed to take his own life and was charged with second-degree murder. The parents of his murdered wife chose to forgive their son-in-law, and stood by him during his trial, visited him in prison, and even invited him to stay in their home when he was released until he could get settled.

Some years later I talked with his mother-in-law—the wife's mother. I asked her how she was able to forgive her son-in-law as she and her husband had. Her answer was clear. She said, "We felt we didn't have an option. Jesus doesn't leave any loopholes in what we are to forgive. It was very difficult for us, but we made the decision within hours that, as believers, we had no choice but to forgive. So we made that choice."

I asked her, "What about all your pain? What did you do about that?"

"Oh, forgiving him didn't take away the pain," she answered. "We have spent years working through that pain to where we finally feel that the forgiveness is complete. Yet we knew we couldn't take a chance and not forgive, for that would lead us directly into a life filled with bitterness."

She went on to describe how she and her husband were the beneficiaries of their forgiveness. "When bad things happen to us, the only way we can find freedom is through forgiveness," she added. She was right, and that's why Jesus said what He said.

Talking Together

What are some of the things that are hard for you to forgive? What makes them difficult to forgive? Talk together about any areas of unforgiveness either one of you may be holding on to, and then make the commitment to help each other to begin the process of forgiving.

Praying Together

Lord God, we want to be forgiving people. You know how hard that is for us sometimes. It seems so unnatural to forgive. Help us in those areas where we still hold on to grudges with a spirit of unforgiveness. Give to us a taste of the joy and freedom we can experience when we truly forgive.
Amen.

DAY 4

Forgiveness Can Take Time

But when the fullness of the time had come, God sent forth His Son,
born of a woman, born under the law.
GALATIANS 4:4, *NKJV*

Sometimes we think that it is a sign of spiritual maturity to forgive quickly. We think this because 1 John 1:9 assures us that when "we confess our sins to him, he is faithful and just to forgive us." How long does it take God to forgive? He does it instantly!

We were traveling with another couple and were to be together for a weekend. At about 10 A.M. on Saturday, Nick, the husband, did something that offended his wife, Kay. He caught what he did and quickly asked Kay to forgive him. She looked at him a bit, and then said, "No."

Nick was quick to respond. "Well," he asked, "what time will the forgiveness come?"

Kay looked at her watch, thought a bit, and then answered, "About 5:00."

We looked at each other and we both wondered what this day was going to hold. However, the day went along nicely. As it got closer to 5:00, I thought I'd better watch to see what would happen. About 5:05, Nick said to Kay, "Hey, it's after 5:00. It's time for forgiveness."

Kay thought a bit and then said, "Okay, you're forgiven." They kissed and that was the end of it. I thought to myself, "Hmm, I guess that was a seven-hour offense."

I think Nick and Kay had it right. When Adam and Eve sinned in the garden, God didn't come in and confront them and quickly forgive them. If He had, He would only have been excusing their behavior, and that would have been an invitation for Adam and Eve to disobey again and eat from the other tree.

No, there were consequences, and there was apparently an animal sacrificed, for Adam and Eve now wore clothes made of an animal skin. Eventually the Old Testament sacrificial system was set up as a partial means for people to find forgiveness. Yet the full and complete forgiveness we enjoy today came when Jesus died on the cross and said, "It is finished." God chose to forgive in the garden, but He took His time completing the process. The time between the act and the completion of forgiveness is based on the seriousness of the offense. Sin was serious, so it took thousands of years until the right time came, and then forgiveness was full and complete. We may sometimes need to take our time to forgive, but we still need to be sure to forgive.

Talking Together

Can you think of times when you forgave and then realized you were still in the process? What did you do? Talk together about the time needed sometimes between the offense and the completion of forgiving.

Praying Together

Heavenly Father, we are grateful that You always meant to forgive even though You took Your time completing the process. Sometimes we are too quick to forgive deep hurts and then we wonder why we are still bothered by them. Give us a spirit of discernment to know what is appropriate in the timing of our forgiving.
Amen.

DAY 5

Forgiveness Never Makes a Wrong Right

Well then, should we keep on sinning so that God can show us more and
more kindness and forgiveness? Of course not!

ROMANS 6:1-2

Sometimes when a hurt is deep, or the offense occurred when we were young, we may struggle with forgiveness, thinking that if we forgive we will somehow make the evil act into something that was okay. I think that part of our struggle in this is that we think that when we forgive, it is the other person who benefits from our forgiving. The truth is, the other person doesn't even need to know we have forgiven him or her.

Rudy had always struggled with his memories of his abusive father. He thought he had those memories under control, and then his son was born and a great fear rose up within him that he would somehow repeat the pattern and be abusive with his own son. He determined that this would never happen, but still the fear haunted him, especially as his son entered his twos.

I talked with him about his need to do something to resolve the inner conflict about his father. I pointed out that his ways of coping with the typical two-year-old behavior of his son weren't going to work when his son became a teenager. He needed to do some grief work with his father.

"What's that?" he asked.

I told him that he needed to look honestly at what his father had done, and then to grieve over what his father never was to him that he needed him to be and over what his father was that he shouldn't have been. Then he could begin to forgive him.

I no sooner had the word "forgive" out of my mouth than he almost shouted at me, "Forgive? I'll never forgive that man!"

I asked him why not, and he said that he had always felt that if he forgave his father, it would be like he was saying that what his father had done was okay. I pointed him to Romans 6 and said, "God never makes a wrong right by forgiving. The wrong is always wrong—it's just forgiven."

Talking Together

Have you ever talked with someone who felt like Rudy—that forgiving would make a wrong into a right? How would you help someone who had that belief system?

Praying Together

Dear Lord, we never want to fall into the trap of thinking that forgiveness does away with the wrongness of an act. We know that Adam and Eve paid the consequences for their act, even though they were forgiven. When we struggle with that concept, help us to see that sin always remains sin, even though it is forgiven.
Amen.

DAY 6

Forgiveness Involves Remembering

And I will forgive their wickedness and will never again remember their sins.
JEREMIAH 31:34

The saying "forgive and forget" goes back to thirteenth-century England. It has been deeply ingrained within us that when we forgive, we should also forget. The way I hear this expressed is, "I still remember, so I guess I haven't forgiven." We often think of God as forgiving and forgetting our sins, and Jeremiah says that this is what God will do. He can forgive and forget. However, we, as humans, are destined to forgive and remember, and there is good reason for that.

For one thing, God knows everything, so He doesn't need to learn anything in the process of forgiving. We are limited in our knowledge and need to keep on learning. Therefore, when we forgive, we need to remember, for we need to learn some things in the process.

Dennis had a problem with stretching the truth. He would lie to Elaine, his wife, even when there was no reason for him to lie. As we talked about his behavior, he said that he had always lied as a child, for his mother was an alcoholic and he could never really tell her the truth without it creating some giant problem. Lying was therefore a deeply ingrained pattern in his life.

The real problem was that he had recently become a believer and felt that God was working in this part of his life—that he was learning the importance of being truthful. As he shared this, Elaine began to softly cry. I stopped Dennis and asked her what she was feeling right then.

She answered, "I want to learn to believe him, and I've forgiven him hundreds of times as we've cried together over his lying. But I'm so afraid that if I let my guard down and start to believe him, I'll be hurt again."

She had forgiven and remembered it as a protection against continued hurt and disappointment. Yet now that Dennis was taking more responsibility, it didn't mean that she should forget the past just because she had forgiven him. She needed to remember, but she also needed to be open to the possibility that Dennis was now telling the truth. In fact, her task was almost as hard as Dennis's. Both of them needed to work on some new patterns in their relationship.

Talking Together

What are some of the things you have forgiven in your life that are still hard to forget? What are some of the things you have learned when you have forgiven and remembered?

Praying Together

*Lord, we don't like to remember hurtful things, but we know that we
will remember, so help us to stay in the forgiving frame of mind when
old hurts come to mind. Help us learn the lessons we need to learn as
we forgive and to never forget the enormity of Your forgiveness.*
Amen.

DAY 7

Forgiveness and Reconciliation Are Different

We urge you, as though Christ himself were here pleading with you,
"Be reconciled to God!"

2 CORINTHIANS 5:20

Forgiveness and reconciliation are separate processes, even though we often put them together. In the Jewish teaching of forgiveness, they are one and the same, for one must repent in order to be forgiven. Yet, according to Christ's teaching, they must be separate, for we must always forgive even though sometimes there cannot be reconciliation.

Hopefully, in our marriages, forgiveness and reconciliation go hand in hand, with one leading to the other. Yet even in marriage this is sometimes impossible, for one partner may have hardened his or her heart against either forgiving or repenting. This is often seen after a bitter divorce, or after a betrayal, such as an affair. One person so hardens his or her heart that he or she either refuses to forgive, or does not see any need to repent and show godly sorrow.

Lindsey refused to forgive Mike for once again humiliating her in front of his family. In fact, she had been refusing now for over a year, and she refused to visit with Mike's family if he was going to be there. Needless to say, their marriage was not on a solid footing.

Mike finally said, "I know I've made fun of her with my family, but we all do that with each other. It's nothing. I don't know why she can't just roll with things."

Lindsey reacted by adding, "He's done this for years, and every time I end up crying. I don't know why he doesn't get it. He just doesn't see it, and I'm done with his family!"

There had been forgiveness in the past, but now Lindsey had stopped forgiving. Maybe the forgiveness she had given in the past had been so easy that it really wasn't forgiving—it was simply excusing Mike's behavior. It still seemed like she had a forgiving heart—she just needed to know that in forgiving Mike, she could still stay away from his family. Mike's hardness of heart regarding her hurt made genuine reconciliation on this issue impossible. He needed to make the next move.

It takes only one person to forgive, but both parties must be involved in the healing process if genuine reconciliation is to take place.

Talking Together

Sometimes what was normal in our family-of-origin isn't acceptable with our partner. Have there been any patterns like this in your relationship? What would you say to Mike to help him "get it"? Talk about the difference between forgiveness and reconciliation.

Praying Together

Lord, we never want to harden our hearts to You or to each other. Help us to stay open to the emotions we each experience and to take them seriously. Keep our hearts tender toward each other. We thank You for taking our emotions seriously. Help us in those areas where we may not quite "get it" and may miss what our partner needs.
Amen.

CREATING AN INTENTIONAL MARRIAGE

DAY 1

In the Intentional Marriage, the Couple Always Savors the Sense of Mystery

There are three things that amaze me—no, four things I do not understand:
how an eagle glides through the sky, how a snake slithers on a rock,
how a ship navigates the ocean, how a man loves a woman.

PROVERBS 30:18-19

Modern science has been able to explain the first three of Agur's (the author of Proverbs 30) amazing things. Today, we understand aeronautics and how the shape of the eagle's wings help it glide. We understand how a snake moves and how ships navigate. Yet when it comes to love, no one has been able to define the dynamics of it. I hope they never do.

One way we can describe what is going on in our culture today, with the high rate of divorce, is that people are experimenting with what might be called "monogamous polygamy." By this we mean that people are living monogamously—with one spouse—yet they are doing so with many different spouses, just one at a time.

The alternative is to practice "polygamous monogamy." Here we are talking about having many marriages, but with only one person. I like what this phrase connotes. It is a way to savor the mystery of our partner. You see, we are all growing and changing over time. When we savor the mystery of our partner, we are always excited to discover new things about who he or she is, and to recommit ourselves to what he or she is becoming.

Jan and I look at each other this way. We have been married to each other for over forty-six years. During that time we have changed a lot. We have grown, and we are very different from who we were when we married each other. Over the years we have enjoyed learning new things about each other, and there have been many times when we have consciously or unconsciously recommitted ourselves to each other. That's an example of "polygamous monogamy."

Love needs to be treasured. Most of all, the fact that God loves us unconditionally is to be taken seriously, for we can more easily receive the love from our spouse when we know that regardless of how we grow or change, God does intentionally love each of us, and we can intentionally love each other.

Talking Together

Discuss the concept of "polygamous monogamy." How has your love for one another grown or changed since your wedding?

Praying Together

Almighty God, You are the Creator of all things. You are high above us, and You are so much more than we are. We can only bow before Your majesty. Yet You have chosen to love us and to send Your Son to die for us. Help us to receive Your love—to know that we truly are loved by You. Help us also to never lose the sense of mystery we have about each other.
Amen.

DAY 2

The Intentional Marriage Has Goals

The plans of the godly are just.
PROVERBS 12:5

Marriage is the most important step we can take in this life, apart from our relationship with God. We come to marriage with high expectations. Yet all too many couples become disillusioned and hurt and settle for less than they hoped for, or simply give up and try again.

I asked Eric and Courtney if they had ever set goals for their marriage. They looked at each other and then one of them simply said "no."

"Why not?" I asked. "People set goals for themselves for all kinds of things—income, career, weight, vacations—why not for marriage?"

"I don't really know," answered Courtney. "I guess no one ever suggested it to us and we never thought of it. It makes good sense, though, and I think we should do it."

Their experience isn't really unusual. We often think of love as a passive action—at least when it comes to loving our marriage partner. We talk about "falling in love," which sounds very passive. We don't "choose to love"; we "fall in love." Of course, if we "fall in love," we can also "fall out of love," and that sounds equally passive.

In the intentional marriage, we choose to love. We not only decide we are going to love and to continue to love, we think in terms of what that love will be like a year from now and five years from now. Then we develop a plan to help make that happen. At a conference center where we had a retreat years before, Jan and I spoke at a couples' retreat. A couple came up and said they had not only been at our sessions ten years ago, they had been to this retreat each year for the past fifteen years. I commended them, for they were being intentional about their marriage and about their love for each other.

When we set goals for our marriage relationship, we also look at how to make these goals a reality. We know that sometimes our goals will change, but the plan keeps on working. Plan to attend a couples' retreat once a year, to have a date night each week, and to set aside time each week just to check in with each other. Those three things make a good beginning for a healthy marriage.

Talking Together

What are some of the goals you have for your marriage? Sometimes we have these goals and dreams in our heads, but we don't share them. Talk about it and then come up with a five-year dream for your marriage, and then break that dream down into manageable goals.

Praying Together

Lord Jesus, we are guilty of sometimes thinking that a good marriage just happens. Sometimes we even hesitate to set goals, for that seems to leave out the leading of Your Spirit. Yet we acknowledge that Your Word encourages us to plan. Help us build a plan for our marriage that is motivating, inspiring and workable, and most of all that brings honor and glory to You.

Amen.

DAY 3

An Intentional Marriage Is Built on Mutual Encouragement

Dear brothers and sisters, I close my letter with these last words: Rejoice.
Change your ways. Encourage each other. Live in harmony and peace.
Then the God of love and peace will be with you.

2 CORINTHIANS 13:11

There is power in words of encouragement. We all know how powerful it can be to hear a word of encouragement from someone we love. Encouragement is different from praise. When we praise someone for something, we are focusing on his or her accomplishment. We praise our son for hitting a home run, or for getting As on his report card. We praise our wife for a good dinner, or praise our husband for cleaning out the garage.

While there is nothing really wrong with praising these accomplishments, praise is not as powerful as encouragement. We encourage someone when instead of focusing on the product of what he or she has done, we focus on the process the person went through to get there. For example, we might say to our husband after he has cleaned out the garage, "Wow, that must feel really good to finally get that done."

Notice how that statement helps him focus in on his own feelings, to see if that really does feel good—which I'm sure it does. Praise, without the words of encouragement, might just lead your husband to respond to your thankfulness at a job that is finally finished with a "Yeah, sure." There's no reflection on how it really feels to him.

While there have been many things written about this for parents, I think it is just as valid a concern when it comes to a husband and a wife. A comment after dinner to your wife or husband such as, "That was really tasty tonight, you must have had some fun putting that meal (or dish) together," goes further than a simple, "Thanks, hon." Not to disparage the "Thanks, hon"; the encouragement simply goes further and is a more powerful statement in any relationship, but especially in a marriage.

Encouragement also takes more work than simple praise, for now we need to focus on what we think the other person might have experienced in the process. Try it and see. When Paul told the Corinthians to encourage one another, he was also correcting their critical attitudes. The same thing will happen in our marriages when we encourage each other.

Talking Together

Can you think of times when you have encouraged each other in the way described here? Share how it would feel if your partner took a praise statement and changed it into a word of encouragement for you.

Praying Together

Father, we sometimes get so caught up in the finished product
that we ignore the process. Give us patience with each other and
help us to be an encouragement to our family members,
but most of all to our marriage partner.
Amen.

DAY 4

An Intentional Marriage Is Able to Handle Money Well

But people who long to be rich fall into temptation and are trapped by many foolish and harmful desires that plunge them into ruin and destruction.
1 TIMOTHY 6:9

One of the major problems identified within marriage is money. Most couples that divorce say that their reason for ending the marriage was that they couldn't work out financial issues. It is easy to see what Scripture means when it says, "the love of money is at the root of all kinds of evil" (1 Tim. 6:10). Jesus spoke more about money than about any other subject, and there are more verses in the Bible that relate to money than to any other subject. Why is money such an issue?

I think there are two answers. The first has to do with power. Greg and Colleen were struggling in their marriage. Colleen came to see me, stating that Greg didn't see any problem. As we talked about her concerns, she came down to the issue of priorities in their marriage. "All Greg wants to do is work. He has his own business and has done very well, but he's at his shop twelve to fourteen hours a day, six days a week. He'd be there on Sunday, too, if I hadn't insisted long ago that he go to church with me and the kids."

She hesitated a bit, and then continued, "Now that the kids are grown, he doesn't go to church anymore. I think he worships his money."

"Does he keep you informed about your finances?" I asked.

"Hardly," was her sarcastic response. "I don't even know how much money we have. I know we have some rentals, but I don't know anything else. He gives me a weekly allowance in cash—always has—and never lets me see a checkbook or even have my name on a check."

Greg knew that money equaled power in their marriage, and he wanted all the power, so he kept Colleen away from the finances. If she wanted to buy something beyond what her allowance covered, she had to ask permission. He had all the power.

The other reason money is so important in the Bible is that it becomes an object of worship. Jesus said, "no one can serve two masters . . . You cannot serve both God and money" (Matt. 6:24). We need to be careful about money. It is a barometer of both our devotion to the Lord and our openness to our partner.

Talking Together

How have you handled money in your marriage? Can you talk about money issues without getting defensive? Where did you get your ideas about money? Do either of you feel left out of financial issues?

Praying Together

Lord God, this money thing is not easy. We really need to see it as a test of our loyalty to You and to each other. Where we struggle, we need You. Help us not only to be open with each other but also to be open with You about our attitudes.

Amen.

DAY 5

An Intentional Marriage Is Built on Honoring Each Other

Love each other with genuine affection, and take delight in honoring each other.
ROMANS 12:10

How well do you know your partner? Do you remember how you used to spend hours talking together before you were married? There was so much to find out. Do you remember how you did your research when you bought your first present? You checked with his or her friends to make sure you bought the "right thing." I'm reminded of the wife who sent her husband flowers at his workplace. He was totally embarrassed by her gift. He kept the card, but put the flowers on his secretary's desk and told her not to say where they were from.

In that case, I think she was giving him a message—send me flowers! She did what we so often do: we give to our partner what we wish he or she would give to us, rather than taking the time to honor our partner by finding out what he or she would really like.

One of the foundation blocks for any marriage is the ongoing friendship we share with each other. Friends stay current with each other. Do you know who your partner's best friend is right now? What is his or her favorite flavor of ice cream? Do you know what his or her favorite TV program is? What's stressing your partner right now? Who is his or her favorite relative?

These things change over time, and we honor our partner by listening in the same way we do with our friends. I remember one time when Jan found out something new about me. I don't like surprise parties when I'm the one being surprised. She planned one for me when I finished my graduate program. We had gone out to eat and came home to a dark house. As we walked into the house, it was freezing cold, and I asked rather rudely and quite loudly, "Who left the air on so low?"

Suddenly there was this low voice from another room that said, "Dave, be nice to her." Needless to say, I was surprised when fifty or so people shouted congratulations!

I was a bit embarrassed that I had spoken so harshly to Jan in front of all those people. I certainly hadn't honored her by the way I had spoken to her.

The party was a lot of fun, and part of the fun for everyone was my embarrassment. Jan was honoring me by giving the party, but later said, "I should have known that you would not like to be surprised. That was not a very good way to honor you, was it?" We both learned a lot about honoring each other that day.

Talking Together

How much do you really know about your partner's likes and dislikes? Do you know your mate's favorite movie, or color? Do you know what honors your partner? In what ways do you honor each other? How current are you in your marital friendship?

Praying Together

Lord God, we want to know You better, and we want to stay current with our partners. Help us to find ways to show interest in what is important to our partners. Give us an openness so that we may honor each other more. Help us to hear each other's concerns as we pray together.
Amen.

DAY 6

In an Intentional Marriage, Each Sees His or Her Partner as a Gift from God

Kind words are like honey—sweet to the soul and healthy for the body.
PROVERBS 16:24

Kind words give value to the recipient of those words. There should be an enforceable rule that says husbands and wives have to be careful about what they say about their partner in public. We've all been embarrassed by someone who is "just joking," but is using humor to disparage his or her partner. It seems like everyone can see through the sarcastic comments except the person making them.

Don had a way of using humor to stop Michelle in her tracks as she talked. He had done this several times as they talked to me, and I finally said to him, "Do you know you are putting your wife down when she is saying something you don't seem to like?"

"Oh," he replied, "I'm just kidding. I don't mind what she's saying."

Michelle spoke up and added, "He does that all the time, and his father does it all the time to his mother. I'm really tired of it."

Often we use humor as a weapon, especially in a marriage relationship. It is convenient, for if we are confronted with what we have said, our defense is that we were only joking.

Later in our discussion, Michelle said something directly to Don that he didn't like and he started the same routine of using humor to put her down. He was laughing as he made his comments, but I cut him off quickly, for he clearly was being very hurtful. Again, his defense was, "Oh, I was only kidding."

Sometimes we use humor to cover our own feelings because we feel too vulnerable to be direct in our communication. Or, as with Don, it is what we have seen while growing up, so we think it is normal. Usually it is only when our partner points out the hurt that we see that it is not healthy for the marriage.

Don knew the truth of the proverb that "kind words are like honey," but at some level he also knew that harsh words spoken clearly and directly were scary, for then he might have to be accountable for their consequences. So he found it easier to slip into the pattern that his father used—giving messages indirectly.

There are many ways we can negate the value of our partner. The misuse of humor is one of them. Kind words feel good to both the giver and the receiver, and affirm to each their value as a gift from God.

Talking Together

Have you ever been uncomfortable around someone who was using humor to communicate negative feelings and disrespect? Have there been times when either of you have used humor to communicate negative feelings? What were the consequences? Talk about how you can show that you value each other.

Praying Together

Heavenly Father, help us to understand better the value of the gift You gave each of us by giving us each other. Forgive us for the times when we have tried to communicate the wrong things through humor. Thank You for dealing with us clearly through Your Word, and help us to communicate clearly as well.

Amen.

DAY 7

An Intentional Marriage Is Built on Being Marriage-Centered

But encourage one another daily, as long as it is called Today,
so that none of you may be hardened by sin's deceitfulness.
HEBREWS 3:13, *NIV*

One of the dangers to marriage over time is that we begin to take our partner for granted. The behaviors that used to feel so good are now expected and have lost their punch. If our kids are young, we sometimes are so preoccupied with them that we forget we have a marriage to honor.

I saw a cartoon recently that showed two young boys standing before a doorway to a large house. One boy said to the other, "You'll like my parents; they are very child-centered." That seems to be a high value in our culture today—to be child-centered. I watch many parents take their kids to all kinds of activities. It can be exhausting just listening to kids' schedules these days. It's hard to imagine when children have time to just be kids. I sometimes wonder if parents are reserving time for their marriages.

I would have liked to rewrite that cartoon and have one of the boys say to the other, "Don't mind my parents; they're just very marriage-centered." But then a couple can become too marriage-centered as well. I've had adults tell me they sometimes felt like they were intruding on their parents when they were kids. They wondered where they fit in.

How do we find a balance between being child-centered and being marriage-centered? I think the admonition in Hebrews 3:13 gives us at least part of the answer—we are to encourage each other daily.

I've observed over the years that often in the early stages of marriage, a woman's self-confidence seems to deteriorate, especially after the first child comes. Her husband is receiving affirmation at work; she's changing diapers. He has stimulating conversations with his boss; she talks baby talk with the infant. Perhaps at no other time does she need her husband to encourage her more, and daily, not only for what she does, but most of all for who she is. Furthermore, this should become a regular habit, for once the kids are raised, to stay successful as a married couple we will have to build the rest of our years on a spirit of mutual encouragement.

Talking Together

Think of a time when one or the other of you was able to instantly change his or her demeanor and tone of voice due to some interruption, like a phone call. How could we better control our emotions so that we could more consistently "encourage one another daily"? Talk about what it means to be marriage-centered as a couple.

Praying Together

Almighty Father, we want You to have first place in our marriage-centered relationship. Help us to understand what we need to change in order for that to happen. Help us to encourage each other daily as we each put the other first, as You intended when You created marriage.

Amen.

More Great Devotionals for Couples from
REGAL BOOKS

MOMENTS WITH YOU
365 All-New Devotions for Couples
Dennis and Barbara Rainey
ISBN 978.08307.43841
ISBN 08307.43847

**MOMENTS TOGETHER
FOR COUPLES**
Daily Devotions for Drawing Near to God
and One Another
Dennis and Barbara Rainey
ISBN 978.08307.17545
ISBN 08307.17544

Regal
God's Word for Your World™
www.regalbooks.com